Book 4

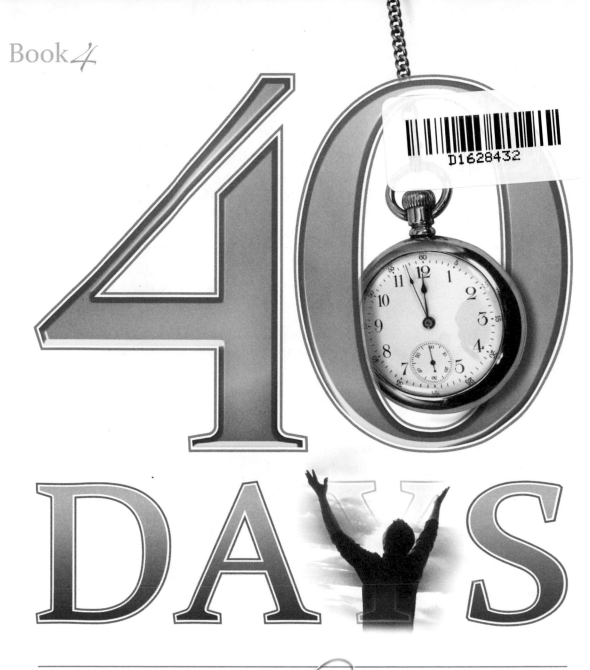

40 DAYS

Prayers *and* Devotions *on* Earth's *Final* Events

DENNIS SMITH

REVIEW AND HERALD® PUBLISHING ASSOCIATION

Since 1861 | www.reviewandherald.com

Also by Dennis Smith:

40 Days: Prayers and Devotions to Prepare for the Second Coming (KJV Edition)
40 Days: Prayers and Devotions to Prepare for the Second Coming (NKJV Edition)
40 Days: Prayers and Devotions to Revive Your Experience With God (Book 2)
40 Days: God's Health Principles for His Last-Day People (Book 3)

To order, call **1-800-765-6955**.
Visit us at **www.reviewandherald.com**
for information on other Review and Herald® products.

Copyright © 2013 by Review and Herald® Publishing Association
Published by Review and Herald® Publishing Association, Hagerstown, MD 21741-1119

Review and Herald® titles may be purchased in bulk for educational, business, fund-raising, or sales promotional use. For information, e-mail SpecialMarkets@reviewandherald.com.

The Review and Herald® Publishing Association publishes biblically based materials for spiritual, physical, and mental growth and Christian discipleship.

This book was
Edited by Kalie Kelch
Copyedited by Amy Prindle
Cover Designed by Ron Pride / Review and Herald® Design Center
Interior Designed by Emily Ford / Review and Herald® Design Center
Cover art by © Thinkstock.com
Typeset: Times New Roman 11.6/15.6

Unless otherwise noted, all scriptures quoted in this book are from the King James Version.

Texts credited to NIV are from the *Holy Bible, New International Version.* Copyright © 1973, 1978, 1984, 2011 by Biblica, Inc. Used by permission. All rights reserved worldwide.

Verses marked TLB are taken from *The Living Bible,* copyright © 1971 by Tyndale House Publishers, Wheaton, Ill. Used by permission.

PRINTED IN U.S.A.
17 16 15 14 13   5 4 3 2

Library of Congress Cataloging-in-Publication Data
Smith, Dennis Edwin, 1944-   .
  40 days : prayers and devotions on earth's final events / by Dennis Smith.
     p. cm.
  "Book 4."
  1. End of the world—Prayers and devotions. 2. End of the world—Biblical teaching. 3. Seventh-Day Adventists—Prayers and devotions. 4. General Conference of Seventh-Day Adventists—Doctrines. I. Title. II. Title: Forty days.
  BT877.S65 2013
  242'.2—dc23
                    2012032282
  ISBN 978-0-8280-2688-8

Contents

A NOTE FROM THE AUTHOR ~ 5
INTRODUCTION ~ 7

Day 1   Earth's Final Events Are Fast Approaching ~ 11
Day 2   An Irrefutable Sign ~ 13
Day 3   Who Shall Be Able to Stand? ~ 15
Day 4   The Seal of God ~ 17
Day 5   How Do You Receive the Seal of God? ~ 19
Day 6   The Promise of the Spirit ~ 21
Day 7   Let Christ Live Out His Righteous Life in You ~ 23
Day 8   The Judgment ~ 25
Day 9   A Prophetic Sequence of Events—Part 1 ~ 27
Day 10   A Prophetic Sequence of Events—Part 2 ~ 29
Day 11   The Latter Rain of the Spirit ~ 31
Day 12   The Church's Laodicean Condition ~ 33
Day 13   Let Jesus In ~ 35
Day 14   The Wise Virgins ~ 37
Day 15   The Foolish Virgins ~ 39
Day 16   Gold, White Raiment, and Eye Salve ~ 41
Day 17   Revival and Reformation ~ 43
Day 18   The Shaking of God's Church—Part 1 ~ 45
Day 19   The Shaking of God's Church—Part 2 ~ 47
Day 20   The Battle of Armageddon ~ 49
Day 21   Miracles ~ 51
Day 22   The Antichrist ~ 53
Day 23   The Mark of the Beast ~ 55
Day 24   The Loud Cry and Little Time of Trouble ~ 57
Day 25   Living Without Christ as Mediator ~ 59
Day 26   The Time of Trouble or Tribulation ~ 61
Day 27   The Seven Last Plagues ~ 63
Day 28   1,000 Years of Peace ~ 65
Day 29   The Great White Throne Judgment ~ 67
Day 30   The New Earth ~ 69
Day 31   Exchanging Death for Life ~ 71

Day 32   Exchanging Unrighteousness for Righteousness ~ 73

Day 33   God's Word and Earth's Final Events ~ 75

Day 34   Prayer and Earth's Final Events ~ 77

Day 35   Fellowship and Earth's Final Events ~ 79

Day 36   Experiencing God's Love ~ 81

Day 37   The Importance of Health Principles ~ 83

Day 38   Spirit Baptism and Righteousness by Faith Required ~ 85

Day 39   The Mystery of God Finished ~ 87

Day 40   With God ~ 89

Appendix A   Daily Prayer List ~ 91

Appendix B   Activities to Show You Care ~ 92

Appendix C   Suggested Greeting for Prayer Contact ~ 93

Appendix D   After the 40 Days of Prayer and Devotional Studies ~ 94

Appendix E   Father's Love Letter ~ 95

A Note *From the Author*

I became a Seventh-day Adventist Christian as the result of studying Bible prophecy. There was a time when I doubted the existence of God and had no faith in the Bible. God used Bible prophecy to convince me there is a God, and that the Bible is His divinely inspired Word. So for the first 30 years as a Christian (most of that time as a pastor) I enjoyed the study of prophecy. Then in September 1999 the Lord led me to study the teaching on the baptism of the Holy Spirit and, later, righteousness by faith in Christ alone.

Once I began to understand the biblical teachings on the baptism of the Holy Spirit and righteousness by faith, I began to question why the Lord had led me to study prophecy for more than 30 years. After all, the baptism of the Holy Spirit and righteousness by faith seemed to be the answer to how God's people are to be ready for Christ's second coming.

As I reflected on these things, the Lord clarified why He had led me as He had. I began to understand how the baptism of the Holy Spirit and righteousness by faith are essential if we are to really understand the prophecies of last-day events. It wasn't enough simply to understand the Bible prophecies. No, one must also understand and experience the baptism of the Holy Spirit and righteousness by faith in order to be faithful to Christ during the climactic events of earth's history.

This fourth *40 Days* devotional is the result of God bringing together in my understanding these two great themes: Bible prophecy and the experience in the Spirit and Christ one must have to be ready for earth's final events.

I pray that this devotional will be a blessing to all who read it, and that God will use it to prepare His people for Christ's soon return.

Introduction

This 40-days-of-study-and-prayer devotional is the fourth in the series of 40-day devotionals. As with the first three 40-day devotionals, this is designed to prepare God's church for Christ's second coming as well as reach out to others in preparation for that glorious event. This preparation begins with church members who are willing to commit to 40 days of prayer and devotional study to develop a closer personal relationship with Jesus Christ and reach out to five individuals of whom the Lord has put upon their hearts to pray for every day.

Why Focus on Last-Day Events?

The devotional studies in this book focus on the events that are to take place just prior to Christ's second coming, and the relationship we must have with Christ to be ready for those events and Christ's return. Personal study of God's Word, prayer, genuine Christian fellowship, understanding and experiencing the baptism of the Holy Spirit, and righteousness by faith are essential elements in the lives of God's last-day people. I personally believe Christ is coming soon, and it is important that every Christian understands the events they will soon be facing, as well as the underlying issues involved.

A Double Blessing

If you want to develop a closer relationship with Jesus in preparation for earth's final events, and if you desire to reach out to those whom God has put upon your heart who have either once known the truth of God's Word and have slipped away, or have never known the warning message God is giving to prepare the world for Christ's soon return, then this 40 days of devotional studies and prayer is for you.

The first task is to create a prayer list of family members, friends, coworkers, etc. A "Daily Prayer List" (Appendix A) is provided for this purpose. During the 40 days of this study you are to pray for them every day and choose items from the "Activities to Show You Care" list (Appendix B) to reach out to those you are praying for as the Lord directs you. Appendix C is a "Suggested Greeting" to use when you call those on your prayer list to inform them you will be praying for them during the next 40 days. Use it to ask them what they want you to pray for. The 40 days of this study will become a double blessing as you grow closer to God and reach out to others.

Prayer's Central Role

Prayer is the most powerful force on earth. Prayer is essential for one's own personal spiritual growth and is the most effective means of reaching others for Christ. Concerning prayer and the Christian's spiritual growth, Ellen White wrote:

"Prayer is the breath of the soul. It is the secret of spiritual power. No other means of grace can be substituted, and the health of the soul be preserved. Prayer brings the heart into immediate contact with the Well-spring of life, and strengthens the sinew and muscle of the religious experience. Neglect the exercise of prayer, or engage in prayer spasmodically, now and then, as seems convenient, and you lose your hold on God. The spiritual faculties lose their vitality, the religious experience lacks health and vigor" (*Gospel Workers*, pp. 254, 255).

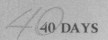

She also recognized the necessity of prayer in leading others to Christ:

"Through much prayer you must labor for souls, for this is the only method by which you can reach hearts. It is not your work, but the work of Christ who is by your side, that impresses hearts" (*Evangelism,* p. 342).

"The Lord will hear our prayers for the conversion of souls " (*Messages to Young People,* p. 315).

As you prayerfully consider the suggested ways to reach out to those for whom you are praying, you will not only be praying for them, you will also be working to bring them closer to Christ and His church. God will bless your efforts when you pray for and work for those on your prayer list. He will not only use you to win others to Christ, He will also draw you closer to Himself. Ellen White understood this double blessing when she wrote:

"As you work to answer your own prayers, you will find that God will reveal Himself unto you. . . . Begin now to reach higher and still higher. Prize the things of heaven above earthly attractions and inducements. . . . Learn how to pray; learn how to bear a clear and intelligent testimony, and God will be glorified in you" (*The Upward Look*, p. 256).

"Their persevering prayers will bring souls to the cross. In cooperation with their self-sacrificing efforts Jesus will move upon hearts, working miracles in the conversion of souls" (*Testimonies for the Church*, vol. 7, p. 27).

In order to facilitate the prayer emphasis in this book, there is a Prayer Activity section at the end of each day's devotional. This section gives a suggested prayer focus for the day, which is related to the corresponding devotional subject and those on your prayer list.

If you are using this devotional study in preparation for a Visitors' Sabbath and/or evangelistic meetings at the end of the 40 days, those programs should be included in the prayer focus each day. As already mentioned, prayer is an important component of unleashing the power of the Holy Spirit, which will be evident in the increased attendance at Visitors' Sabbath and/or evangelist meetings because of your effort to reach out to people and pray for them.

Fellowship

Christian fellowship is designed by God to assist His children in their personal spiritual growth and victory over temptation. We weren't created to stand alone. Paul commands us to pray for one another (Eph. 6:18). John tells us that we are called by God to fellowship (1 John 1:3), and Christ said He is especially present when two or three believers fellowship together (Matt. 18:20). Therefore it is highly recommended that you choose a fellow Christian to discuss the devotional with each day, and pray for one another and for those you are reaching out to for Christ. This can be done via phone call or in person.

Focus on the Baptism of the Holy Spirit

After His resurrection, Jesus told His disciples that they were to wait to receive the baptism of the Holy Spirit before they went forth to proclaim the gospel to the world:

"And, being assembled together with them, commanded them that they should not depart from Jerusalem, but wait for the promise of the Father, which, saith he, ye have heard of me. For John truly baptized with water; but ye shall be baptized with the Holy Ghost not many days hence. . . . But ye shall receive power, after that the Holy Ghost is come upon you: and ye shall be witnesses unto me both in Jerusalem, and in all Judaea, and in Samaria, and unto the uttermost part of the earth" (Acts 1:4-8).

Even though they had spent the past three and a half years with Christ and had seen and participated in a ministry of miracles, they were not ready to witness for Him. They were to wait to receive the "power." After they received the baptism of the Holy Spirit, which took place on the day of Pentecost, they were "empowered" as never before to witness for Christ.

"And when the day of Pentecost was fully come, they were all with one accord in one place. And suddenly there came a sound from heaven as of a rushing mighty wind, and it filled all the house where they were sitting. And there appeared unto them cloven tongues like as of fire, and it sat upon each of them. And they were all filled with the Holy Ghost, and began to speak with other tongues, as the Spirit gave them utterance" (Acts 2:1-4).

Because the baptism of the Holy Spirit, also called the infilling of the Spirit, is so vital to our personal spiritual growth and our witness to others, this important teaching is interwoven throughout the devotional studies. You will have opportunity to better understand and experience the biblical teaching on the baptism of the Holy Spirit, as well as see its relationship to other vital biblical teachings.

An Amazing Spiritual Adventure

By choosing to participate in the 40 days of study and prayer, you are entering into an amazing and blessed adventure with the Lord. You will experience a deeper relationship with Christ as you apply the spiritual principles presented, and you will see the Lord use you to draw others closer to Himself in preparation for His soon return. As you fellowship with your prayer partner and the others participating in the 40 days of prayer and devotional study, you will experience a deeper Christian love and unity with other believers, which will also play an important role in your personal spiritual growth after you have completed the 40 days.

In order to get the most from the 40 days of study and prayer, it is recommended that this be the first thing you do in the morning. It may require rising a little earlier, but the effort will be well rewarded. If you ask the Lord to wake you so you can have some quality time with Him, He will hear and answer your prayer. Concerning Christ's devotional life, Ellen White wrote:

"Daily He received a fresh baptism of the Holy Spirit. In the early hours of the new day the Lord awakened Him from His slumbers, and His soul and His lips were anointed with grace, that He might impart to others. His words were given Him fresh from the heavenly courts, words that He might speak in season to the weary and oppressed" (*Christ's Object Lessons*, p. 139).

Christ will do the same for you if you ask Him. He very much desires to anoint you with His Spirit in preparation for each new day. This 40-day devotional study is designed to facilitate just that—a daily anointing of God's Spirit for personal spiritual growth and witnessing for Christ.

Other Resources

Note: Information on how to conduct a 40-days program of devotional study and prayer in your church is available at www.40daysdevotional.com. A free, downloadable Instruction Manual is located on the Web site.

The 40 devotionals are also prepared to work along with Light America Mission, a program of personal spiritual growth through study of God's Word, prayer, training, and community outreach to share the three angels' messages.

"*Nothing* but the baptism of the Holy Spirit can bring up the church to its right position, and prepare the people of God for the fast approaching conflict."

—*Manuscript Releases, vol. 2, p. 30*

Day 1

Earth's Final Events Are Fast Approaching

This 40-day devotional focuses on earth's final events. Christians throughout the centuries have believed that earth's final events are soon to come upon them and that Christ is about to return. That certainly seemed to be the case in the early church. Because of this incorrect belief, Paul wrote:

"Now we beseech you, brethren, by the coming of our Lord Jesus Christ, and by our gathering together unto him, that ye be not soon shaken in mind, or be troubled, neither by spirit, nor by word, nor by letter as from us, as that the day of Christ is at hand. Let no man deceive you by any means: for that day shall not come, except there come a falling away first, and that man of sin be revealed, the son of perdition; who opposeth and exalteth himself above all that is called God, or that is worshipped; so that he as God sitteth in the temple of God, shewing himself that he is God" (2 Thess. 2:1-4).

It seems that some were teaching in Paul's day that Christ was about to return. In light of this, a logical question would be "How do we know that Christ is about to return in *our* day?" Hopefully that question will be answered throughout this book. I will give a partial answer in today's devotional.

Jesus cautioned His disciples:

"And ye shall hear of wars and rumours of wars: see that ye be not troubled: for all these things must come to pass, but the end is not yet. For nation shall rise against nation, and kingdom against kingdom: and there shall be famines, and pestilences, and earthquakes, in divers places" (Matt. 24:6, 7).

Since the twentieth century there have been "world" wars and conflicts between countries and regions in many parts of the world. To make matters worse, some nations have the power to actually destroy the world several times over using their nuclear weapons. Hundreds of thousands die every year from famine and starvation. The pestilence of disease periodically erupts in pandemic proportions, resulting in massive loss of life. The fear of a pandemic looms on the horizon when one considers how rapidly disease can spread because of interpersonal contact during worldwide travel. In recent years tsunamis, earthquakes, tornadoes, hurricanes, and floods have killed hundreds of thousands. These events are statistically increasing each year and are becoming more and more destructive.

Paul warned of these phenomena when he wrote:

"But of the times and the seasons, brethren, ye have no need that I write unto you. For yourselves know perfectly that the day of the Lord so cometh as a thief in the night. For when they shall say, Peace and safety; then sudden destruction cometh upon them, as travail upon a woman with child; and they shall not escape. But ye, brethren, are not in darkness, that that day should overtake you as a thief" (1 Thess. 5:1-4).

A woman about to give birth experiences the travail of birth pains more intensely and closer together as the birth itself grows nearer. So also, as we approach Christ's second coming, earth's final destructive events will occur more frequently and with more destructive power. That is exactly what we are seeing happen today.

Jesus also gave this warning:

"And there shall be signs in the sun, and in the moon, and in the stars; and upon the earth distress of nations, with perplexity; the sea and the waves roaring; men's hearts failing them for fear, and for looking

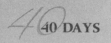

after those things which are coming on the earth: for the powers of heaven shall be shaken. And then shall they see the Son of man coming in a cloud with power and great glory" (Luke 21:25-27).

Just before Jesus returns, the sea and waves will be especially destructive. There will also be astronomical signs in the sun, moon, and stars that will create destruction, as the very "powers of heaven shall be shaken." These events that will befall the earth will cause great fear in the hearts of all people and perplexity among national leaders. These final catastrophic events take place immediately prior to Christ's return: "And then shall they see the Son of man coming in a cloud with power and great glory."

These destructive forces that were foretold through Bible prophecy indicate that earth's final events are upon us and Christ is about to return. God has given us

these warning signs because He wants us to be ready for that event. Throughout history God has always warned His children of what is to come so they can know in advance what to expect:

"Surely the Lord God will do nothing, but he revealeth his secret unto his servants the prophets" (Amos 3:7).

God has revealed to Christians the "secrets" of earth's final events. But it is one thing to know about earth's final events and quite another to be ready for them. One important aspect of being ready for these events is daily experiencing the baptism of the Holy Spirit. Ellen White wrote:

"Nothing but the baptism of the Holy Spirit can bring up the church to its right position, and prepare the people of God for the fast approaching conflict" (*Manuscript Releases*, vol. 2, p. 30).

Personal Reflection and Discussion

1. Why were Christians in the apostle Paul's day incorrect in their belief that Jesus was about to return?

_____

_____

2. What signs did Jesus give as evidence of His imminent return? _____

_____

3. To whom does God reveal the signs of Christ's coming? _____

_____

4. Why does God reveal His secrets to His prophets? _____

_____

5. What daily experience must you have to be ready for earth's final events? _____

_____

Prayer Activity

● **Call your prayer partner and discuss the devotional with him or her.**
● **Pray with your prayer partner:**
    (1) for God to lead you into the truth of the signs of earth's final events
    (2) for God to baptize you with His Holy Spirit
    (3) for those on your prayer list

Day 2

An Irrefutable Sign

When Christians tell non-Christians about the signs of Christ's return, many simply reply, "Well, there have always been earthquakes, wars, pestilence, and famines." They don't realize it, but they are actually fulfilling a prophecy of the apostle Peter:

"Knowing this first, that there shall come in the last days scoffers, walking after their own lusts, and saying, Where is the promise of his coming? for since the fathers fell asleep, all things continue as they were from the beginning of the creation" (2 Peter 3:3, 4).

It is true the signs mentioned by Jesus as indications of His return have been occurring for centuries. The difference today is that these signs are happening more frequently and are more destructive.

Yet there is one sign that no one can refute. Daniel records this sign that the angel gave in chapter 12 of his book:

"But thou, O Daniel, shut up the words, and seal the book, even to the time of the end: many shall run to and fro, and knowledge shall be increased" (Dan. 12:4).

The first application of this verse applies to people "running to and fro" in the Bible. By studying the Word of God, biblical knowledge increases. That is happening today.

However, there is another application of this verse that predicts that humanity will run to and fro in this world, and general knowledge will increase during the last days of earth's history. Concerning humankind running to and fro, almost every year sees increases in worldwide travel. For example, in 2010 there were 786.7 million airline passengers in the United States. That figure far exceeds the number of passengers in previous decades. The same applies to travel in general. In the nineteenth century many never left the county or the state they were born in. Today one would have difficulty finding someone with such a limited amount of travel experience.

The increase of knowledge in our day was first brought to my attention when I was sitting in a thermodynamics class one day during my senior year at Colorado State University. For some reason the professor mentioned that we are further from the 1800s technologically and knowledge-wise than the 1800s were from the days of the Roman Empire. At that time I was just beginning to give serious consideration to what the Bible taught. So when my engineering professor made that statement, it caught my attention.

Knowledge is indeed increasing exponentially; statistics verify it. It is estimated that a week's worth of reading the New York *Times* contains more information than a person would likely have come across in a lifetime in the eighteenth century. We live in the information age. According to the Geneva Association, at the end of 2009 the global data volume reached 800 exabytes. If that weren't enough, in 2009 a company in Japan "successfully tested a fiber-optic cable" that pushed "14 trillion bits per second down a single strand of fiber. That's 2,660 CDs or 210 million phone calls per second" (Daniel Kinnaman, *District Administration,* January 2009). This rate is currently tripling every six months and is expected to do so for the next 20 years.

It is predicted that by 2013 a supercomputer will be built that exceeds the computational capabilities of the human brain. Some people are predicting that by 2049 a $1,000 computer will exceed the computational

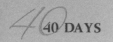

capabilities of the entire human race on earth.

Other fields, such as astrophysics, particle physics, quantum mechanics, medical advances—the list could go on and on—are growing extremely rapidly. Knowledge in all fields of study is increasing at amazing rates. If anyone denies this, he or she simply does not know the facts.

Dear reader, earth's final events are fast approaching. Knowledge of science and technology is good; however, a saving knowledge of Jesus Christ is the most important thing you will ever study.

"And this is life eternal, that they might know thee the only true God, and Jesus Christ, whom thou hast sent" (John 17:3).

"The fear of the Lord is the beginning of wisdom: a good understanding have all they that do his commandments: his praise endureth for ever" (Ps. 111:10).

Remember, the Bible gives a description of those who are ready for Jesus' return:

"Here is the patience of the saints: here are they that keep the commandments of God, and the faith of Jesus" (Rev. 14:12).

If you want to be ready for heaven, make sure this verse describes you.

Personal Reflection and Discussion

1. What objection do many non-Christians make when they are told about the signs of Christ's return?

_____

_____

2. What New Testament prophecy are they actually fulfilling? _____

_____

3. What did the angel mean when he told Daniel that human beings would run to and fro in the time of the end? _____

_____

4. What did the angel mean when he said knowledge would increase? _____

_____

5. List some of the areas where knowledge is increasing rapidly today. _____

_____

Prayer Activity

- **Call your prayer partner and discuss the devotional with him or her.**
- **Pray with your prayer partner:**
    - **(1) for God to help you understand the truth of Daniel's prophecy**
    - **(2) for God to daily lead you into a renewed saving relationship with Jesus Christ**
    - **(3) for God to baptize you with His Holy Spirit**
    - **(4) for those on your prayer list**

Day 3

Who Shall Be Able to Stand?

The catastrophic events taking place on Planet Earth today indicate that Christ is about to return. Christians have been longing for this great event throughout the centuries. Paul described this event with these words:

"Looking for that blessed hope, and the glorious appearing of the great God and our Saviour Jesus Christ" (Titus 2:13).

The second coming of Jesus will affect every human being on earth. John the revelator wrote:

"Behold, he cometh with clouds; and every eye shall see him" (Rev. 1:7).

And in the book of Matthew we read:

"When the Son of man shall come in his glory, and all the holy angels with him, then shall he sit upon the throne of his glory" (Matt. 25:31).

This will be a wonderful experience for those anticipating Christ's return. Paul described the scene:

"The Lord himself shall descend from heaven with a shout, with the voice of the archangel, and with the trump of God: and the dead in Christ shall rise first: then we which are alive and remain shall be caught up together with them in the clouds, to meet the Lord in the air: and so shall we ever be with the Lord" (1 Thess. 4:16, 17).

The righteous of all ages who have died in Christ will be resurrected and meet Jesus in the air. Then the righteous who are alive will be "caught up" to Jesus. Jesus' literal return was foretold by angels at Christ's ascension, following His resurrection:

"And when he had spoken these things, while they beheld, he was taken up; and a cloud received him out of their sight. And while they looked stedfastly toward heaven as he went up, behold, two men stood by them in white apparel; which also said, Ye men of Galilee, why stand ye gazing up into heaven? this same Jesus, which is taken up from you into heaven, shall so come in like manner as ye have seen him go into heaven" (Acts 1:9-11).

This event will have a very different effect on the unrighteous, or "wicked." They are destroyed by the "brightness" of Christ's coming, as told in 2 Thess. 2:

"And then shall that Wicked be revealed, whom the Lord shall consume with the spirit of his mouth, and shall destroy with the brightness of his coming: even him, whose coming is after the working of Satan with all power and signs and lying wonders, and with all deceivableness of unrighteousness in them that perish; because they received not the love of the truth, that they might be saved" (verses 8-10).

Those who are not ready when Christ returns will be terrified by this great, earthshaking event. John described their reaction with these words:

"And the kings of the earth, and the great men, and the rich men, and the chief captains, and the mighty men, and every bondman, and every free man, hid themselves in the dens and in the rocks of the mountains; and said to the mountains and rocks, Fall on us, and hide us from the face of him that sitteth on the throne, and from the wrath of the Lamb: for the great day of his wrath is come; and who shall be able to stand?" (Rev. 6:15-17).

The question asked by those seeking to hide from the presence of Christ at His second coming is very significant. They ask, "Who shall be able to stand" or survive this great event? We must also ask ourselves, "How can we be ready to stand in the presence of Christ, in all His glory, and not be consumed?" The answer is given in Revelation 7:

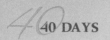

"And after these things I saw four angels standing on the four corners of the earth, holding the four winds of the earth, that the wind should not blow on the earth, nor on the sea, nor on any tree. And I saw another angel ascending from the east, having the seal of the living God: and he cried with a loud voice to the four angels, to whom it was given to hurt the earth and the sea, saying, Hurt not the earth, neither the sea, nor the trees, till we have sealed the servants of our God in their foreheads" (verses 1-3).

Those who receive the "seal" of God are the ones who will be ready to meet Jesus when He returns.

Personal Reflection and Discussion

1. What does Paul call the second coming of Jesus? _____

_____

2. How many people will see Jesus when He returns? _____

_____

3. When Jesus returns, what will happen to God's people who have died and are asleep in the grave?

_____

_____

4. When Jesus returns, what will happen to God's people who are still living? _____

_____

5. What will happen to the unrighteous or wicked when Jesus returns? _____

_____

6. What does Revelation 7 say the righteous have that enables them to be ready for Christ's second coming? _____

_____

Prayer Activity

● **Call your prayer partner and discuss the devotional with him or her.**
● **Pray with your prayer partner:**
  (1) for God to lead you to receive the seal of God
  (2) for God to enable you to be among His people when Jesus returns
  (3) for God to baptize you with His Holy Spirit
  (4) for those on your prayer list

Day 4

The Seal of God

Yesterday's devotional ended with the Bible verse that answers the question "Who will be able to stand in the presence of Christ in all His glory and not be consumed?" The answer was found in Revelation 7:

"And after these things I saw four angels standing on the four corners of the earth, holding the four winds of the earth, that the wind should not blow on the earth, nor on the sea, nor on any tree. And I saw another angel ascending from the east, having the seal of the living God: and he cried with a loud voice to the four angels, to whom it was given to hurt the earth and the sea, saying, Hurt not the earth, neither the sea, nor the trees, till we have sealed the servants of our God in their foreheads" (verses 1-3).

In these verses we see several important teachings. First, the angels are holding back the winds of destruction until God's people are ready for these events. Second, we learn that the angel who prepares God's people comes from the east. In Bible prophecy God's glory comes from the east (Eze. 43:2).

This is the angel who completes the work among God's people, which will enable them to reflect God's glory and thus fulfill Revelation 18:1:

"And after these things I saw another angel come down from heaven, having great power; and the earth was lightened with his glory."

God's glory refers to His character and name. When Moses asked to see God's glory, God said this:

"I will make all my goodness pass before thee, and I will proclaim the name of the Lord before thee; and will be gracious to whom I will be gracious, and will shew mercy on whom I will shew mercy" (Ex. 33:19).

This is why those who proclaim the three angels' messages in power and are ready for Christ's return are described as having the Father's name in their foreheads:

"And I looked, and, lo, a Lamb stood on the mount Sion, and with him an hundred forty and four thousand, having his Father's name written in their foreheads" (Rev. 14:1).

They are reflecting Christ's character, thus filling the earth with God's glory. Also notice that they are described as being on Mount Zion, which is in Jerusalem. This is all symbolic language. For when one accepts Christ, they are portrayed as coming to Mount Zion and Jerusalem (heavenly Jerusalem):

"But ye are come unto mount Sion, and unto the city of the living God, the heavenly Jerusalem, and to an innumerable company of angels, to the general assembly and church of the firstborn, which are written in heaven, and to God the Judge of all, and to the spirits of just men made perfect, and to Jesus the mediator of the new covenant" (Heb. 12:22-24).

This same kind of symbolism is used to describe God's call to His people to come out of symbolic Babylon:

"And he cried mightily with a strong voice, saying, Babylon the great is fallen, is fallen. . . . And I heard another voice from heaven, saying, Come out of her, my people, that ye be not partakers of her sins, and that ye receive not of her plagues" (Rev. 18:2-4).

Also note that this angel's loud and powerful cry to come out of Babylon takes place as God's people are perfectly reflecting Christ's character; they have the Father's name in their foreheads (verse 1).

The Bible tells us that it is by the Holy Spirit that we are sealed and able to reflect God's character:

"And grieve not the holy Spirit of God, whereby ye are sealed unto the day of redemption" (Eph. 4:30).

Paul tells us that it is the Holy Spirit who writes

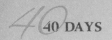

God's law on our hearts: "Forasmuch as ye are manifestly declared to be the epistle of Christ ministered by us, written not with ink, but with the Spirit of the living God; not in tables of stone, but in fleshy tables of the heart" (2 Cor. 3:3).

Therefore, those who receive the seal of God will have the Ten Commandments, which were originally written on "tables of stone," manifest in their life—including the seventh-day Sabbath of the fourth commandment. This is also the new covenant promise:

"For finding fault with them, he saith, Behold, the days come, saith the Lord, when I will make a new covenant with the house of Israel and with the house of Judah. . . . For this is the covenant that I will make with the house of Israel after those days, saith the Lord; I will put my laws into their mind, and write them in their hearts: and I will be to them a God, and they shall be to me a people" (Heb. 8:8-10).

Therefore it is the Holy Spirit who fulfills the new covenant promise to write God's Ten Commandments on the hearts and minds (foreheads) of the believers. Since God's law is a transcript of His character, His followers are reflecting the character of God in their life.

In summary, those who are able to stand in the presence of Christ when He returns in all His glory are those who come out of Babylon, receive the seal of God, and have God's Ten Commandments written in their hearts and minds by the Holy Spirit. This means the Father's name or character is reflected in their lives. For this to happen, God's people must experience the full reviving power of the Holy Spirit.

"A revival of true godliness among us is our greatest and most urgent of all our needs. To seek this should be our first work. . . . A revival need be expected only in answer to prayer" (*Selected Messages*, book 1, p. 121).

Personal Reflection and Discussion

1. Why are the angels holding back the winds of destruction? _____
_____

2. What does receiving the seal of God do for His people? _____
_____

3. How does the Christian receive the seal of God? _____
_____

4. What does the seal of God have to do with the Ten Commandments?_____
_____

5. According to Ellen White, what is the church's greatest need and how is that need met? _____
_____

Prayer Activity

- **Call your prayer partner and discuss the devotional with him or her.**
- **Pray with your prayer partner:**
    - **(1) for God to baptize you with His Spirit**
    - **(2) for God to bring revival into your life and the church**
    - **(3) for those on your prayer list**

How Do You Receive the Seal of God?

We saw in yesterday's devotional that those who are ready to meet Jesus will have the seal of God in their foreheads, which is also referred to as having God's name in their foreheads and reflecting His glory (character) in their lives. They will experience a daily baptism of the Holy Spirit and His reviving power. A very important question is, then, "How do you receive the seal of God?"

In his letter to the Ephesians, the apostle Paul described how we are sealed:

"And grieve not the holy Spirit of God, whereby ye are sealed unto the day of redemption" (Eph. 4:30).

It is through the Holy Spirit that one is sealed and prepared for Christ's return. Jesus described this special experience of the Spirit in the believer's life during a speech of encouragement to His disciples:

"And I will pray the Father, and he shall give you another Comforter, that he may abide with you for ever; even the Spirit of truth; whom the world cannot receive, because it seeth him not, neither knoweth him: but ye know him; for he dwelleth with you, and shall be in you" (John 14:16, 17).

Here Jesus told the disciples that the day was coming when the Holy Spirit would be available to dwell "in" all believers. That took place on the day of Pentecost, when the Holy Spirit was poured out and all were "filled," or baptized, with the Spirit:

"And when the day of Pentecost was fully come, they were all with one accord in one place. And suddenly there came a sound from heaven as of a rushing mighty wind, and it filled all the house where they were sitting. And there appeared unto them cloven tongues like as of fire, and it sat upon each of them. And they were all filled with the Holy Ghost, and began to speak with other tongues, as the Spirit gave them utterance" (Acts 2:1-4).

From the day of Pentecost onward the Holy Spirit was available to fill, or baptize, each believer. This experience is so important that Paul commanded that each follower of Christ keep on being filled with the Spirit every day:

"And be not drunk with wine, wherein is excess; but be filled with the Spirit" (Eph. 5:18).

The Greek verb that translates "be filled" is a continuous action verb, meaning to "keep on being filled" with the Spirit.

Jesus is our example in all things. We read in Luke's Gospel about Christ Himself receiving the baptism of the Spirit in His life:

"Now when all the people were baptized, it came to pass, that Jesus also being baptized, and praying, the heaven was opened, and the Holy Ghost descended in a bodily shape like a dove upon him, and a voice came from heaven, which said, Thou art my beloved Son; in thee I am well pleased" (Luke 3:21, 22).

Immediately following Christ's baptism He is described as being "filled" with the Spirit:

"And Jesus being full of the Holy Ghost returned from Jordan, and was led by the Spirit into the wilderness" (Luke 4:1).

And once in the wilderness, Jesus faced His greatest temptations:

"Being forty days tempted of the devil. And in those days he did eat nothing: and when they were ended, he afterward hungered" (verse 2).

Jesus was not ready to face those temptations until

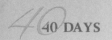

He was filled with the Spirit, for it was through the Holy Spirit that Jesus was sealed by the Father:

"Labour not for the meat which perisheth, but for that meat which endureth unto everlasting life, which the Son of man shall give unto you: for him hath God the Father sealed" (John 6:27).

The same is true of those living in the last days. God's people are not ready for Satan's final and greatest temptations until they, too, are sealed by the Spirit.

We know from Scripture that the antichrist, who is also called the "son of perdition" (2 Thess. 2:3) or "lawless one" (NIV), will seek to lead all to disobey God's law during earth's final events. Hence, since the last issue in the great conflict that began in heaven (Rev. 12:7) will be over the law of God, it is essential that God's people have His law firmly established in their life by the Holy Spirit writing it on their hearts (2 Cor. 3:3). They must receive the seal of God in order to be continually faithful to Him and be ready for Christ's return.

The angels are holding back the winds of temptation and destruction until God's people become a Spirit-filled people and are empowered to live a life of faithful obedience to Christ. They will proclaim the third angel's message (Rev. 14:9-11), calling God's people out of Babylon by the mighty loud cry of the Spirit (Rev. 18:1-4).

Personal Reflection and Discussion

1. How does one receive the seal of God? _____

_____

2. What did Jesus say the Holy Spirit would do in the Christian's life on the day of Pentecost?_____

_____

3. What did Paul command all believers to experience every day? _____

_____

4. What did the baptism of the Holy Spirit do in Jesus' life?_____

_____

5. What experience must every Christian have in order to be ready for Satan's last great temptations?

_____

_____

Prayer Activity

● **Call your prayer partner and discuss the devotional with him or her.**
● **Pray with your prayer partner:**
    (1) for God to baptize you with His Spirit
    (2) for God to continue to bring revival in your life and the church
    (3) for God to write His law on your heart
    (4) for those on your prayer list

Day 6

The Promise of the Spirit

In yesterday's devotional we studied the considerable importance of being filled with the Spirit. Today we will look more closely at what the Bible teaches about this promise of the Spirit. Through the prophet Joel, God gave a wonderful promise:

"Be glad then, ye children of Zion, and rejoice in the Lord your God: for he hath given you the former rain moderately, and he will cause to come down for you the rain, the former rain, and the latter rain in the first month" (Joel 2:23).

In this verse God promised two great outpourings of the Holy Spirit: the former or early rain and the latter rain. Joel went on to write:

"And ye shall know that I am in the midst of Israel, and that I am the Lord your God, and none else: and my people shall never be ashamed. And it shall come to pass afterward, that I will pour out my spirit upon all flesh; and your sons and your daughters shall prophesy, your old men shall dream dreams, your young men shall see visions" (verses 27, 28).

Here we are told that the former rain of the Spirit would come soon after the "I Am" appeared in the "midst of Israel," which referred to Christ's first advent (John 8:58). John the Baptist spoke of this great Holy Spirit event (Matt. 3:11). Jesus also proclaimed this promise:

"I have come to bring fire on the earth, and how I wish it were already kindled!" (Luke 12:49, NIV).

"And, being assembled together with them, commanded them that they should not depart from Jerusalem, but wait for the promise of the Father, which, saith he, ye have heard of me. For John truly baptized with water; but ye shall be baptized with the Holy Ghost not many days hence" (Acts 1:4, 5).

This former or early rain of the Spirit, which Jesus called the baptism of the Spirit, began to fall on the earth on the day of Pentecost, which Peter spoke of in his sermon that day:

"But Peter, standing up with the eleven, lifted up his voice, and said unto them, Ye men of Judaea, and all ye that dwell at Jerusalem, be this known unto you, and hearken to my words: For these are not drunken, as ye suppose, seeing it is but the third hour of the day. But this is that which was spoken by the prophet Joel; and it shall come to pass in the last days, saith God, I will pour out of my Spirit upon all flesh: and your sons and your daughters shall prophesy, and your young men shall see visions, and your old men shall dream dreams: and on my servants and on my handmaidens I will pour out in those days of my Spirit; and they shall prophesy" (Acts 2:14-18).

When Jesus was about to leave the earth and ascend back to heaven, He told His disciples of this wonderful promise of the Spirit:

"And I will pray the Father, and he shall give you another Comforter, that he may abide with you for ever; even the Spirit of truth; whom the world cannot receive, because it seeth him not, neither knoweth him: but ye know him; for he dwelleth with you, and shall be in you. I will not leave you comfortless: I will come to you" (John 14:16-18).

In this discourse Jesus told the disciples that it was through the baptism of the Holy Spirit that He would come to them and live in them. It is through this same Spirit baptism that He lives most fully in us today. Paul clearly understood this reality:

"I am crucified with Christ: nevertheless I live; yet not I, but Christ liveth in me" (Gal. 2:20).

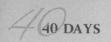

"Christ in you, the hope of glory" (Col. 1:27).

This was such an important experience in Paul's teaching that he commanded the believers in Ephesus to "be not drunk with wine, wherein is excess; but be filled with the Spirit" (Eph. 5:18). He used the Greek verb form for "filled," meaning a continuous action. So Paul instructs us to "keep on being filled" with the Spirit every day.

Ellen White also understood the importance of daily seeking the baptism of the Spirit:

"What we need is the baptism of the Holy Spirit. Without this, we are no more fitted to go forth to the world than were the disciples after the crucifixion of their Lord" (*Selected Messages,* book 1, p. 411).

"Impress upon all the necessity of the baptism of the Holy Spirit, the sanctification of the members of the church, so that they will be living, growing, fruit-bearing trees of the Lord's planting" (*Testimonies for the Church,* vol. 6, p. 86).

Personal Reflection and Discussion

1. When did the prophet Joel foretell that the former rain of the Spirit would be poured out? _____
_____
_____

2. What did Jesus say about the baptism, or former rain, of the Spirit? _____
_____
_____

3. Who lives in us through the baptism of the Holy Spirit? _____
_____
_____

4. How often should we seek the baptism of the Holy Spirit? _____
_____
_____

Prayer Activity

● **Call your prayer partner and discuss the devotional with him or her.**
● **Pray with your prayer partner:**
    (1) for God to baptize you with His Holy Spirit
    (2) for God to continue to bring revival in your life and the church
    (3) for Jesus to live in you through the Holy Spirit
    (4) for the individuals on your prayer list

Day 7

Let Christ Live Out His Righteous Life in You

When the angels let go of the winds of destruction and Satan brings his greatest temptations upon God's people, they must be able to withstand this onslaught. They must remain faithful to Christ during the most trying time in earth's history, which is called the "time of trouble," or tribulation. This is why those who go through that time are described as having the "patience of the saints: here are they that keep the commandments of God, and the faith of Jesus" (Rev. 14:12).

God, in His Word, calls for perfect righteousness in the life of His followers, even during the earth's most trying time. Paul wrote of this to the believers in Rome: "Likewise reckon ye also yourselves to be dead indeed unto sin, but alive unto God through Jesus Christ our Lord. Let not sin therefore reign in your mortal body, that ye should obey it in the lusts thereof. Neither yield ye your members as instruments of unrighteousness unto sin: but yield yourselves unto God, as those that are alive from the dead, and your members as instruments of righteousness unto God. For sin shall not have dominion over you: for ye are not under the law, but under grace" (Rom. 6:11-14).

However, because of our sinful condition, it is impossible for us to live a perfectly righteous, obedient life. Paul described this impossibility:

"For I know that in me (that is, in my flesh,) dwelleth no good thing: for to will is present with me; but how to perform that which is good I find not. . . . I find then a law, that, when I would do good, evil is present with me. For I delight in the law of God after the inward man: but I see another law in my members, warring against the law of my mind, and bringing me into captivity to the law of sin which is in my members" (Rom. 7:18-23).

This is why understanding and experiencing the baptism of the Holy Spirit is so important. It is through the baptism of the Holy Spirit that Jesus lives in the believer (John 14:16-18). Because of this reality, when we are tempted we can simply ask Jesus, who lives in us, to give us His obedience. He can do this because He overcame every temptation for us (Heb. 4:15), as He knew it was impossible for us, in our sinful nature, to overcome by simply trying hard to obey.

Therefore, when we are tempted, we are to "look to Jesus" for our victory (Heb. 12:1, 2). When we are tempted to be impatient, we can ask Jesus to give us His patience. When we are tempted to be angry and unforgiving, we can ask Jesus to give us His peace and forgiveness. If we choose to turn from a temptation and ask Jesus for His victory over that temptation, believing He will do that for us, He will. This is why Ellen White wrote: "The only defense against evil is the indwelling of Christ in the heart through faith in His righteousness" (*The Desire of Ages*, p. 324).

Paul clearly understood that Christ was the only way to victory:

"I am crucified with Christ: nevertheless I live; yet not I, but Christ liveth in me: and the life which I now live in the flesh I live by the faith of the Son of God, who loved me, and gave himself for me" (Gal. 2:20).

When Christ died on the cross, the power of our sinful nature was broken (Rom. 6:6). That is why Paul wrote that he was "crucified" with Christ and yet still alive. However, it was not Paul who was actually living the obedient life—it was Christ living in him. He lived the obedient life by trusting Christ to live out His obedience in him.

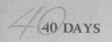

Christ is to be the very life force of the Christian. This is why, in other Scriptures, Paul wrote that we are saved by His life (Rom. 5:10), Christ is our life (Col. 3:4), and to live is Christ (Phil. 1:21). This is also why Ellen White wrote:

"He who has not sufficient faith in Christ to believe that He can keep him from sinning has not the faith that will give him an entrance into the kingdom of God" (*Selected Messages*, book 3, p. 360).

Remember, it is Christ who can keep us faithful and obedient by living out His life in us:

"Now unto him that is able to keep you from falling, and to present you faultless before the presence of his glory with exceeding joy" (Jude 24).

Personal Reflection and Discussion

1. What kind of obedience does God's justice demand? _____

_____

_____

2. Is it possible for the Christian to perfectly obey God by trying his or her hardest? _____

_____

_____

3. How does Christ live in the Christian? _____

_____

_____

4. Describe how the Christian is to obtain victory over temptation and sin: _____

_____

_____

Prayer Activity

● **Call your prayer partner and discuss the devotional with him or her.**
● **Pray with your prayer partner:**
  (1) **for God to baptize you with His Holy Spirit**
  (2) **for God to continue to bring revival in your life and the church**
  (3) **for Jesus to live out His obedient life in you**
  (4) **for the individuals on your prayer list**

The Judgment

A very significant event that must take place before Jesus returns is the judgment. Every case must be decided as to who will be taken to heaven with Jesus when He returns and who will not.

"He that is unjust, let him be unjust still: and he which is filthy, let him be filthy still: and he that is righteous, let him be righteous still: and he that is holy, let him be holy still. And, behold, I come quickly; and my reward is with me, to give every man according as his work shall be" (Rev. 22:11, 12).

No one escapes God's judgment:

"For we must all appear before the judgment seat of Christ; that every one may receive the things done in his body, according to that he hath done, whether it be good or bad" (2 Cor. 5:10).

Nothing in the lives of human beings is hid from God:

"For God shall bring every work into judgment, with every secret thing, whether it be good, or whether it be evil" (Eccl. 12:14).

The standard God uses to judge all inhabitants of the earth is His Ten Commandments:

"For whosoever shall keep the whole law, and yet offend in one point, he is guilty of all. For he that said, Do not commit adultery, said also, Do not kill. Now if thou commit no adultery, yet if thou kill, thou art become a transgressor of the law. So speak ye, and so do, as they that shall be judged by the law of liberty" (James 2:10-12).

Daniel described the judgment in the following way:

"I beheld till the thrones were cast down, and the Ancient of days did sit, whose garment was white as snow, and the hair of his head like the pure wool: his throne was like the fiery flame, and his wheels as burning fire. A fiery stream issued and came forth from before him: thousand thousands ministered unto him, and ten thousand times ten thousand stood before him: the judgment was set, and the books were opened" (Dan. 7:9, 10).

Here we see that the judgment began when Christ appeared before the Father, the Ancient of Days. Following the symbols of the Old Testament sanctuary service, God's throne is represented as being in the Most Holy Place where the ark of God was located. It contained the Ten Commandments with God's presence manifest above the ark. Once a year, on the Day of Atonement, the high priest entered the Most Holy Place in a service to cleanse the sanctuary of sin. This was considered a day of judgment, because the sins of Israel came up before God. If their sins had been confessed, the sins could be cleansed from the sanctuary by the symbolic, pure blood of Christ, ministered by the high priest. If the sins of an individual were not covered by the blood, they were cut off from the people. The Day of Atonement is still considered the most holy day in the Jewish calendar.

According to Daniel 8 and 9 the actual judgment, described in Daniel 7 (quoted above), began on October 22, 1844. On that day Christ, our high priest (Heb. 8:1, 2), entered the Most Holy Place of the heavenly sanctuary to intercede in behalf of His people. All who have accepted Christ as their Savior are covered by His blood. Their sins are cleansed, and they are clothed in the robe of His justifying and sanctifying righteousness. Their names remain in the book of life:

"He that overcometh, the same shall be clothed in white raiment; and I will not blot out his name out of

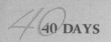

the book of life, but I will confess his name before my Father, and before his angels" (Rev. 3:5).

It is important to remember that in the Old Testament, when a sinner brought his sacrificial lamb to the priest as a sin offering, the priest did not inspect the sinner—he inspected the lamb. All who have accepted the Lamb of God as their sacrifice will pass inspection every time and have nothing to fear in the judgment.

The work of the judgment will be completed just before Jesus returns for His people. Once this work is complete, God's people must live without Christ serving as mediator in the heavenly sanctuary. This is why it is absolutely essential that those living at that time must understand and experience the daily baptism of the Holy Spirit, as well as Christ's justifying and sanctifying righteousness. They will have learned how to let Christ live out His life in and through them 100 percent of the time.

Ellen White describes their spiritual condition with these words:

"All true obedience comes from the heart. It was heart work with Christ. And if we consent, He will so identify Himself with our thoughts and aims, so blend our hearts and minds into conformity to His will, that when obeying Him we shall be but carrying out our own impulses. The will, refined and sanctified, will find its highest delight in doing His service. When we know God as it is our privilege to know Him, our life will be a life of continual obedience. Through an appreciation of the character of Christ, through communion with God, sin will become hateful to us" (*The Desire of Ages*, p. 668).

Personal Reflection and Discussion

1. **What must take place in the heavenly sanctuary before Jesus returns?** _____

_____

2. **How many will face God's judgment?** _____

3. **What law is the standard to which everyone's life is compared in the judgment?** _____

_____

4. **Why does the Christian not have to fear the judgment?** _____

_____

5. **What kind of life must the Christian be living after the judgment ends, just before Jesus returns?**

_____

_____

Prayer Activity

● **Call your prayer partner and discuss the devotional with him or her.**
● **Pray with your prayer partner:**
   (1) for God to baptize you with His Holy Spirit
   (2) for God to continue to bring revival in your life and the church
   (3) for Jesus to live out His obedient life in you
   (4) for the individuals on your prayer list

A Prophetic Sequence of Events—Part 1

For those who are living when Jesus returns it is absolutely essential to have learned how to let Jesus live out His obedient, righteous life in and through them. Just like Peter, they must be able to say:

"Grace and peace be multiplied unto you through the knowledge of God, and of Jesus our Lord, according as his divine power hath given unto us all things that pertain unto life and godliness, through the knowledge of him that hath called us to glory and virtue: whereby are given unto us exceeding great and precious promises: that by these ye might be partakers of the divine nature, having escaped the corruption that is in the world through lust. And beside this, giving all diligence, add to your faith virtue; and to virtue knowledge; and to knowledge temperance; and to temperance patience; and to patience godliness; and to godliness brotherly kindness; and to brotherly kindness charity. For if these things be in you, and abound, they make you that ye shall neither be barren nor unfruitful in the knowledge of our Lord Jesus Christ. But he that lacketh these things is blind, and cannot see afar off, and hath forgotten that he was purged from his old sins. Wherefore the rather, brethren, give diligence to make your calling and election sure: for if ye do these things, ye shall never fall: for so an entrance shall be ministered unto you abundantly into the everlasting kingdom of our Lord and Saviour Jesus Christ" (2 Peter 1:2-11).

Why is complete victory over temptation and sin so essential for those who are ready to meet Jesus when He returns? The answer to that question becomes clear when we understand the events that take place just prior to Christ's return. Daniel describes the following:

"And at that time shall Michael stand up, the great prince which standeth for the children of thy people: and there shall be a time of trouble, such as never was since there was a nation even to that same time: and at that time thy people shall be delivered, every one that shall be found written in the book" (Dan. 12:1).

In this verse God gives us a significant sequence of events. Michael standing up refers to Christ completing His work of judgment in the Most Holy Place of the heavenly sanctuary. As soon as this work of judgment is complete, the time of trouble or tribulation comes upon this earth. At the end of this period of time Christ will return and deliver His people from destruction. Those delivered are those whose names are in the book of life as a result of the judgment Christ will have just completed.

Another verse that gives a sequence of these final events is found in Peter's sermon in Acts 3:

"Repent ye therefore, and be converted, that your sins may be blotted out, when the times of refreshing shall come from the presence of the Lord; and he shall send Jesus Christ, which before was preached unto you" (verses 19, 20).

These two verses call God's people to "repent and be converted," referring to a total commitment to Jesus Christ in every aspect of life. It is a call to complete surrender to Jesus and victory through Jesus. It is only those who experience the complete justifying and sanctifying righteousness of Christ whose sins will be "blotted out" at the end of the judgment. This complete victory is necessary in order to benefit from the "times of refreshing," which is the latter rain of the Spirit.

Concerning this, Ellen White wrote:

"I saw that many were neglecting the preparation

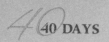

so needful, and were looking to the time of 'refreshing' and the 'latter rain' to fit them to stand in the day of the Lord, and to live in His sight. Oh, how many I saw in the time of trouble without a shelter! They had neglected the needful preparation, therefore they could not receive the refreshing that all must have to fit them to live in the sight of a holy God" (*Christian Experience and Teachings of Ellen White*, p. 112).

"I saw that none could share the 'refreshing,' unless they obtain the victory over every besetment, over pride, selfishness, love of the world, and over every wrong word and action" (*ibid.*, p. 113).

Complete victory through Christ and the latter rain of the Spirit enable God's people to stand in the presence of Christ, in all His glory, when He returns.

Personal Reflection and Discussion

1. List the sequence of events Daniel describes in Daniel 12:1: _____

_____

_____

2. List the sequence of events in Peter's sermon in Acts 3:19, 20: _____

_____

_____

3. What experience is described in 1 Peter 1:1-11 that the Christian must have? _____

_____

_____

4. What experience did Ellen White say the Christian must have in order to receive the latter rain of the Spirit and be ready for Christ's return? _____

_____

_____

Prayer Activity

● **Call your prayer partner and discuss the devotional with him or her.**
● **Pray with your prayer partner:**
   (1) **for God to baptize you with His Holy Spirit**
   (2) **for God to continue to bring revival in your life and the church**
   (3) **for God to lead you to experience Christ's justifying and sanctifying righteousness**
   (4) **for the individuals on your prayer list**

A Prophetic Sequence of Events—Part 2

In yesterday's devotional we read passages in the books of Daniel and Acts about what God's last-day people must do in order to experience the latter rain of the Spirit, have their sins blotted out at the end of the judgment, make it through the time of trouble victoriously, and be ready for Christ's return. Today we will consider another Bible prophecy that teaches the same truth. Malachi wrote:

"Behold, I will send my messenger, and he shall prepare the way before me: and the Lord, whom ye seek, shall suddenly come to his temple, even the messenger of the covenant, whom ye delight in: behold, he shall come, saith the Lord of hosts. But who may abide the day of his coming? and who shall stand when he appeareth? for he is like a refiner's fire, and like fullers' soap: and he shall sit as a refiner and purifier of silver: and he shall purify the sons of Levi, and purge them as gold and silver, that they may offer unto the Lord an offering in righteousness. Then shall the offering of Judah and Jerusalem be pleasant unto the Lord, as in the days of old, and as in former years" (Mal. 3:1-4).

Malachi's statement that the Lord shall "suddenly come to his temple" refers to Christ entering the Most Holy Place in the heavenly sanctuary to begin the work of judgment. This prepares the way for Him to return to earth to deliver His people at the end of the time of trouble. This is why the questions are asked, "Who may abide the day of his coming? Who shall stand when he appears?" The answer: those who enter into the refining process Malachi describes will be ready for Christ's return. That is, those who understand and experience the baptism of the Holy Spirit, Christ's justifying and sanctifying righteousness, and the latter rain of the Spirit.

This process of purification from sin enables God's people to offer to God an "offering in righteousness," which refers to Christ's righteousness being fully manifest in their life. Christ's righteousness is the only righteousness that is acceptable to God, since "all our righteousnesses are as filthy rags" (Isa. 64:6) in God's sight. Only Christ's righteousness is a "pleasant" offering to God.

Ellen White wrote of this truth:

"Those who are living upon the earth when the intercession of Christ shall cease in the sanctuary above are to stand in the sight of a holy God without a mediator. Their robes must be spotless, their characters must be purified from sin by the blood of sprinkling. Through the grace of God and their own diligent effort they must be conquerors in the battle with evil. While the investigative judgment is going forward in heaven, while the sins of penitent believers are being removed from the sanctuary, there is to be a special work of purification, of putting away of sin, among God's people upon earth. This work is more clearly presented in the messages of Revelation 14.

"When this work shall have been accomplished, the followers of Christ will be ready for his appearing. 'Then shall the offering of Judah and Jerusalem be pleasant unto the Lord, as in the days of old, and as in former years.' Malachi 3:4. Then the church which our Lord at His coming is to receive to Himself will be a 'glorious church, not having spot, or wrinkle, or any such thing.' Ephesians 5:27. Then she will look 'forth as the morning, fair as the moon, clear as the sun, and terrible as an army with banners.' Song of Solomon 6:10" (*The Great Controversy*, p. 425).

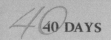

Hence, we are living in very serious times. Earth's final events are fast approaching, and Christ is about to come. All who are ready to meet Him must enter into the purifying process Malachi described and learn how to let Christ live out His obedient, righteous life in and through them. Ellen White described the experience Christ offers to every believer:

"All true obedience comes from the heart. It was heart work with Christ. And if we consent, He will so identify Himself with our thoughts and aims, so blend our hearts and minds into conformity to His will, that when obeying Him we shall be but carrying out our own impulses. The will, refined and sanctified, will find its highest delight in doing His service. When we know God as it is our privilege to know Him, our life will be a life of continual obedience. Through an appreciation of the character of Christ, through communion with God, sin will become hateful to us" (*The Desire of Ages*, p. 668).

Personal Reflection and Discussion

1. What did Malachi mean when he wrote that the Lord shall suddenly come to His temple? _____
_____
_____

2. What was Malachi referring to when he asked the question "Who shall stand when He appears?"
_____
_____

3. How did Malachi describe the refining process that each Christian must experience in order to be ready for Christ's return? _____
_____
_____

4. How did Ellen White describe the experience we can have through Christ? _____
_____

Prayer Activity

- **Call your prayer partner and discuss the devotional with him or her.**
- **Pray with your prayer partner:**
    (1) for God to baptize you with His Holy Spirit
    (2) for God to continue to bring revival in your life and the church
    (3) for God to lead you to experience Christ's complete victory in your life
    (4) for the individuals on your prayer list

The Latter Rain of the Spirit

In a previous devotional we studied the early-rain baptism of the Holy Spirit that became available to all believers on the day of Pentecost. The prophet Joel foretold a "latter rain" of the Spirit as well:

"Be glad then, ye children of Zion, and rejoice in the Lord your God: for he hath given you the former rain moderately, and he will cause to come down for you the rain, the former rain, and the latter rain in the first month" (Joel 2:23).

Here we see both the former or early rain and the latter rain of the Spirit prophesied. A logical question would be "When will this latter rain of the Spirit fall upon the church?" The answer is found in Acts 3:

"Repent ye therefore, and be converted, that your sins may be blotted out, when the times of refreshing shall come from the presence of the Lord; and he shall send Jesus Christ, which before was preached unto you" (verses 19, 20).

Peter tells us that the "times of refreshing," or latter rain of the Spirit, will come during the time that sins are blotted out. This, then, refers to the time that the judgment ends. Hence, as Christ is completing His mediatory work in the heavenly sanctuary, the latter rain of the Spirit will be poured out. This outpouring is necessary for God's delivering power to be fully experienced in the lives of His people, and for the final call to come out of Babylon (Rev. 18:2-5) and go forth in the great power of the Spirit.

The latter rain enables God's people to make it through the time of trouble victoriously and remain faithful to God. It also prepares them to stand in Christ's presence, in all His glory, when He returns. That is why Peter followed his statement about the latter rain with the declaration "And he shall send Jesus Christ."

It is important to realize that one must experience the full benefits of the early-rain baptism of the Holy Spirit in order to benefit from the latter rain of the Spirit. We learn this from the analogy of agriculture in the Middle East. When the crops were planted, the early-rain showers enabled them to grow into a significant level of maturity. Then, when the latter-rain showers fell, it completed the growth process, making them ready for the harvest. If the early-rain showers did not do its work, the crops received no benefit from the latter-rain showers.

Hence, those who benefit from the latter rain of the Spirit will have already grown to a significant level of maturity in Christ under the early-rain baptism of the Spirit. This is why Peter admonished his listeners to "repent and be converted," which means they must experience full commitment to Jesus Christ, having learned how to let Him live out His righteous obedience in and through them.

Ellen White understood this when she wrote:

"I saw that none could share the 'refreshing,' [latter rain] unless they obtain the victory over every besetment, over pride, selfishness, love of the world, and over every wrong word and action" (*Christian Experience and Teachings of Ellen White*, p. 113).

"The latter rain, ripening earth's harvest, represents the spiritual grace that prepares the church for the coming of the Son of man. But unless the former rain has fallen, there will be no life; the green blade will not spring up. Unless the early showers have done their work, the latter rain can bring no seed to perfection" (*The Faith I Live By*, p. 333).

"Unless we are daily advancing in the exemplification of the active Christian virtues, we shall not recognize the manifestations of the Holy Spirit in the latter rain. It may be falling on hearts all around us, but we shall not discern or receive it" (*Testimonies to Ministers,* p. 507).

That last statement is a serious warning. When the latter rain of the Spirit begins to fall, there will be two groups in the church: those who are prepared to receive it because of their spiritual growth under the early rain baptism of the Spirit, and those who are not prepared to receive it. Because of the times in which we are living, we must take seriously our need to understand and experience the early-rain baptism of the Holy Spirit, as well as Christ's justifying and sanctifying righteousness. Only then will we benefit from the latter rain of the Spirit and be ready for Christ's return.

Personal Reflection and Discussion

1. **What two outpourings of the Holy Spirit did Joel prophecy about?** _____

_____

_____

2. **Which experience in the Spirit is the early or former rain?** _____

_____

_____

3. **What experience must the Christian have in Christ to benefit from the latter rain?** _____

_____

_____

4. **What experience did Ellen White say the Christian must have in order to receive the latter rain?**

_____

_____

_____

Prayer Activity

- Call your prayer partner and discuss the devotional with him or her.
- Pray with your prayer partner:
    (1) for God to baptize you with His Holy Spirit
    (2) for God to continue to bring revival in your life and the church
    (3) for God to lead you to experience the full victory in Christ under the power of the early-rain baptism of the Spirit
    (4) for the individuals on your prayer list

Day 12

The Church's Laodicean Condition

In the previous devotionals we have seen the absolute necessity of growing into the full maturity of Christ under the early and latter rain of the Spirit. However, if something doesn't change, the church today will not be ready to experience the last-day events. The Bible describes today's church as being in a Laodicean condition, according to the book of Revelation:

"And unto the angel of the church of the Laodiceans write; These things saith the Amen, the faithful and true witness, the beginning of the creation of God; I know thy works, that thou art neither cold nor hot: I would thou wert cold or hot. So then because thou art lukewarm, and neither cold nor hot, I will spue thee out of my mouth" (Rev. 3:14-16).

The situation is so serious that those who remain in this "lukewarm" condition will be lost when Jesus returns, which is indicated by God stating, "I will spue thee out of my mouth."

The sad truth is that those in Laodicea are unaware of their condition:

"Because thou sayest, I am rich, and increased with goods, and have need of nothing; and knowest not that thou art wretched, and miserable, and poor, and blind, and naked" (Rev. 3:17).

The parable of the 10 virgins describes Laodicean Christians:

"Then shall the kingdom of heaven be likened unto ten virgins, which took their lamps, and went forth to meet the bridegroom. And five of them were wise, and five were foolish. They that were foolish took their lamps, and took no oil with them: but the wise took oil in their vessels with their lamps. While the bridegroom tarried, they all slumbered and slept. And at midnight there was a cry made, Behold, the bridegroom cometh; go ye out to meet him. Then all those virgins arose, and trimmed their lamps. And the foolish said unto the wise, Give us of your oil; for our lamps are gone out. But the wise answered, saying, Not so; lest there be not enough for us and you: but go ye rather to them that sell, and buy for yourselves. And while they went to buy, the bridegroom came; and they that were ready went in with him to the marriage: and the door was shut. Afterward came also the other virgins, saying, Lord, Lord, open to us. But he answered and said, Verily I say unto you, I know you not" (Matt. 25:1-12).

The foolish virgins in the parable are not ready when the bridegroom comes, and subsequently they are told, "I know you not" (verse 12). These foolish virgins did not have the extra oil the wise virgins had. This oil represents of the baptism of the Holy Spirit.

Ellen White described the foolish virgins in the following way:

"The name 'foolish virgins' represents the character of those who have not the genuine heart-work wrought by the Spirit of God. The coming of Christ does not change the foolish virgins into wise ones. . . . The state of the church represented by the *foolish virgins is also spoken of as the Laodicean state*" (in *Review and Herald*, Aug. 19, 1890; italics supplied).

Note that the foolish virgins and the Laodicean Christians are one and the same. Ellen White went on to write:

"The class represented by the foolish virgins are not hypocrites. They have a regard for the truth, they have advocated the truth, they are attracted to those who believe the truth; but they have not yielded them-

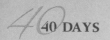

selves to the Holy Spirit's working. . . . The class represented by the foolish virgins have been content with a superficial work. They do not know God. . . . Their service to God degenerates into a form" (*Christ's Object Lessons*, p. 411).

Therefore it is essential that Christians today understand God's warning to the Laodicean church, which represents the Christian church in our day. If we do not heed the warning, we will be counted among the foolish virgins who refuse to come out of the Laodicean condition and thus will not be ready for Christ's second coming. According to the parable, the only way to come out of the Laodicean condition is to understand and experience the baptism of the Holy Spirit, having the "oil" that the foolish virgins do not have.

Personal Reflection and Discussion

1. How does God describe the Laodicean condition?_____
_____
_____

2. What happens to those who do not come out of the Laodicean condition? _____
_____
_____

3. What is the relationship between those in Laodicea and the foolish virgins? _____
_____
_____

4. What do the wise virgins have that distinguishes them from the foolish virgins?_____
_____
_____

Prayer Activity

- Call your prayer partner and discuss the devotional with him or her.
- Pray with your prayer partner:
    (1) for God to baptize you with His Holy Spirit
    (2) for God to continue to bring revival in your life and the church
    (3) for God to bring you out of any Laodicean condition in your life
    (4) for the individuals on your prayer list

Day 13

Let Jesus In

We saw in yesterday's devotional that God gives a very serious warning to those in Laodicea, which describes the church's condition just prior to Christ's second coming. Those who do not come out of their Laodicean condition will be lost. God ends this warning with an appeal:

"Behold, I stand at the door, and knock: if any man hear my voice, and open the door, I will come in to him, and will sup with him, and he with me. To him that overcometh will I grant to sit with me in my throne, even as I also overcame, and am set down with my Father in his throne" (Rev. 3:20, 21).

God's appeal to the Laodiceans is to let Jesus into their lives. An important question would then be "How do we let Jesus fully into our life?" Jesus gives us the answer in John 14:16-18:

"And I will pray the Father, and he shall give you another Comforter, that he may abide with you for ever; even the Spirit of truth; whom the world cannot receive, because it seeth him not, neither knoweth him: but ye know him; for he dwelleth with you, and shall be in you. I will not leave you comfortless: I will come to you."

In these verses Jesus was referring to the Holy Spirit being poured out, filling His followers with the baptism of the Holy Spirit on the day of Pentecost. It is important to notice that Jesus also indicates that when they received the baptism of the Holy Spirit, they were also receiving Him more fully. He said, "I will come to you." Jesus comes and lives in His followers most fully as they daily receive the baptism of the Holy Spirit.

It is also key that Jesus, in Revelation 3:20, 21, made a connection between letting Him in and overcoming sin, even as He overcame. It is as we learn to let Jesus live out His obedience in us that, when we are tempted, we will experience His victory in our life. Paul described this victorious experience when he wrote:

"I am crucified with Christ: nevertheless I live; yet not I, but Christ liveth in me: and the life which I now live in the flesh I live by the faith of the Son of God, who loved me, and gave himself for me" (Gal. 2:20).

Fully experiencing Christ in one's life and learning how to let Jesus manifest His victory over temptation and sin are essential for those ready to meet Him. John described the people possessing this readiness:

"Beloved, now are we the sons of God, and it doth not yet appear what we shall be: but we know that, when he shall appear, we shall be like him; for we shall see him as he is" (1 John 3:2).

Those ready to meet Jesus will be just like Him in character, claiming victory over temptation and sin, authority, etc. Why is this the case? It is because it is actually Jesus Himself that is living out His victory and authority in and through them.

Why is this experience so essential in being ready for Christ's return? First, Christians will have to live during the time of trouble without a mediator, since Christ will have completed His mediator work of the investigative judgment. Plus, they will have to stand in the presence of Christ when He returns, in all His glory, and not be consumed by the brightness of His coming:

"And then shall appear the sign of the Son of man in heaven: and then shall all the tribes of the earth mourn, and they shall see the Son of man coming in the clouds of heaven with power and great glory" (Matt. 24:30).

"And then shall that Wicked be revealed, whom

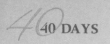

the Lord shall consume with the spirit of his mouth, and shall destroy with the brightness of his coming" (2 Thess. 2:8).

Those alive when Jesus returns will be ready to meet Him only by coming out of their Laodicean condition. They do this by letting Jesus live in them, daily receiving the baptism of the Holy Spirit, which is the "oil" the wise virgins are described as having. As they daily grow through Christ living out His life and obedience in them, they will be continually reflecting the character of Christ and will be able to stand in His presence, in all His glory, and not be consumed.

"Now unto him that is able to keep you from falling, and to present you faultless before the presence of his glory with exceeding joy" (Jude 24).

Personal Reflection and Discussion

1. What does Jesus invite those in Laodicea to do? _____

_____

_____

2. How does one let Jesus fully into their life?_____

_____

_____

3. How did Jesus say He would come to them after He ascended to the Father? _____

_____

_____

4. How will those who let Jesus fully into their life, through daily receiving the baptism of the Holy Spirit, live an obedient life? _____

_____

_____

Prayer Activity

● **Call your prayer partner and discuss the devotional with him or her.**
● **Pray with your prayer partner:**
    (1) **for God to baptize you with His Holy Spirit**
    (2) **for God to continue to bring revival in your life and in the church**
    (3) **for Jesus to live out His obedient life in you every day**
    (4) **for the individuals on your prayer list**

Day 14

The Wise Virgins

In yesterday's devotional we studied about Laodicea and the foolish virgins. We saw that all who remain in the Laodicean, foolish virgin spiritual condition will not be ready for Christ's second coming.

The wise virgins, on the other hand, have extra oil, which is the baptism of the Holy Spirit. Because of this they come out of their Laodicean condition and experience revival and reformation in preparation for earth's final events. The baptism of the Holy Spirit allows God's law to be written on their hearts by the Spirit:

"Forasmuch as ye are manifestly declared to be the epistle of Christ ministered by us, written not with ink, but with the Spirit of the living God; not in tables of stone, but in fleshy tables of the heart" (2 Cor. 3:3).

They obey God from the heart, which means God has placed within them the desire to obey—it is heart-felt and heart-motivated.

The wise virgins do not obey God's law only because it says to obey—to do this or not to do that. That is merely legalistic obedience. They truly have the desire in their heart to obey God. Ellen White described this obedience from the heart in the following manner:

"All true obedience comes from the heart. It was heart work with Christ. And if we consent, He will so identify Himself with our thoughts and aims, so blend our hearts and minds into conformity to His will, that when obeying Him we shall be but carrying out our own impulses. The will, refined and sanctified, will find its highest delight in doing His service. When we know God as it is our privilege to know Him, our life will be a life of continual obedience. Through an appreciation of the character of Christ, through communion with God, sin will become hateful to us" (*The Desire of Ages*, p. 668).

Note that obedience from the heart leads to consistent obedience. In fact, she said that "when obeying Him we shall be but carrying out our own impulses," and that "our life will be a life of continual obedience" when it comes from the heart.

As covered in yesterday's devotional, in order for Laodicean Christians to come out of their condition and become wise virgin Christians, they must let Jesus into their life in this manner:

"Behold, I stand at the door, and knock: if any man hear my voice, and open the door, I will come in to him, and will sup with him, and he with me" (Rev. 3:20).

This happens only through daily receiving the baptism of the Holy Spirit. Jesus associated this baptism with His coming into our lives when He assured His disciples:

"And I will pray the Father, and he shall give you another Comforter, that he may abide with you for ever; even the Spirit of truth; whom the world cannot receive, because it seeth him not, neither knoweth him: but ye know him; for he dwelleth with you, and shall be in you. I will not leave you comfortless: I will come to you" (John 14:16-18).

Ellen White understood that the Holy Spirit brings the presence of Jesus into our life:

"The work of the holy Spirit is immeasurably great. It is from this source that power and efficiency come to the worker for God; and the holy Spirit is the comforter, *as the personal presence of Christ to the soul*" (in *Review and Herald*, Nov. 29, 1892; italics supplied).

This is why she also wrote,

"Nothing but the baptism of the Holy Spirit can

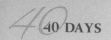

bring up the church to its right position, and prepare the people of God for the fast approaching conflict" (*Manuscript Releases,* vol. 2, p. 30).

When we receive the daily baptism of the Holy Spirit, the presence of Christ will begin to permeate our entire being:

"The sanctification of the soul by the operation of the Holy Spirit is the implanting of Christ's nature in humanity. It is the grace of our Lord Jesus Christ revealed in character, and the grace of Christ brought into active exercise in good works. Thus the character is transformed more and more perfectly after the image of Christ in righteousness and true holiness" (*Selected Messages*, book 3, p. 198).

Hence, daily experiencing the baptism of the Holy Spirit and learning how to let Jesus live out His life of obedience in our own lives are the only means of coming out of our natural Laodicean condition. When we do these things, we experience righteousness by faith in Christ alone. It is urgent that we understand and experience these spiritual steps if we want to make it victoriously through earth's final events and be ready for Christ's return.

Personal Reflection and Discussion

1. What do the wise virgins have that the foolish virgins do not have? _____
_____
_____

2. What does the Holy Spirit do with God's law in the lives of the wise virgins? _____
_____
_____

3. How do the wise virgins let Jesus into their life every day?_____
_____
_____

4. Those ready to meet Jesus must experience the daily baptism of _____
_____**, and righteousness by faith in**_____**for obedience.**

Prayer Activity

● **Call your prayer partner and discuss the devotional with him or her.**
● **Pray with your prayer partner:**
    (1) for God to baptize you with His Holy Spirit
    (2) for God to continue to bring revival in your life and the church
    (3) for God to lead you to experience righteousness by faith in Christ alone, which will bring about obedience in your life
    (4) for the individuals on your prayer list

Day 15

The Foolish Virgins

As we have seen, those who remain in the Laodicean condition and the foolish virgins are one and the same:

"The name 'foolish virgins' represents the character of those who have not the genuine heart-work wrought by the Spirit of God. The coming of Christ does not change the foolish virgins into wise ones. . . . The state of the church represented by the foolish virgins is also spoken of as the Laodicean state" (Ellen G. White, in *Review and Herald*, Aug. 19, 1890).

The tragedy is that the foolish virgin Laodiceans don't realize the dangerous condition they are in and that they will be lost when Jesus returns.

Every Christian, especially those who hold to strong doctrinal beliefs, have a similar danger. For example, since we as Seventh-day Adventists know about the plan of salvation, the Sabbath, the state of the dead, the mark of the beast, and the manner of Christ's second coming, we can fall into the deception that we are safe simply because we know these biblical truths. That is a lie of Satan. Remember, it was those who had the sanctuary and its services in their midst, kept the Sabbath, were careful to return tithes to God, and believed in health reform practices who were the ones that crucified Jesus. They had all those truths, but they didn't know the Messiah who fulfilled those truths. Jesus pointed this out when He prayed:

"And this is life eternal, that they might know thee the only true God, and Jesus Christ, whom thou hast sent" (John 17:3).

Most important is developing a meaningful, intimate relationship with Jesus Christ.

Another danger one can fall into is the deception that involvement in an active and apparently successful ministry for Christ is evidence of knowing Jesus and being ready for His return. Jesus warned against this:

"Not every one that saith unto me, Lord, Lord, shall enter into the kingdom of heaven; but he that doeth the will of my Father which is in heaven. Many will say to me in that day, Lord, Lord, have we not prophesied in thy name? and in thy name have cast out devils? and in thy name done many wonderful works? And then will I profess unto them, I never knew you: depart from me, ye that work iniquity" (Matt. 7:21-23).

You can imagine what a shocking statement that will be to those who appeared to be involved in anointed ministry for Jesus.

Remember, the foolish virgins do not have the extra "oil" the wise virgins have; they are not experiencing the daily baptism of the Holy Spirit. The Spirit's work is to write God's law on the heart:

"Ye are our epistle written in our hearts, known and read of all men: forasmuch as ye are manifestly declared to be the epistle of Christ ministered by us, written not with ink, but with the Spirit of the living God; not in tables of stone, but in fleshy tables of the heart" (2 Cor. 3:2, 3).

Because of this lack of daily infilling of the Spirit, God's law is not being written on their hearts. So their obedience is only a formal, intellectual obedience—not an obedience from the heart.

"The class represented by the foolish virgins are not hypocrites. They have a regard for the truth, they have advocated the truth, they are attracted to those who believe the truth; but they have not yielded themselves to the Holy Spirit's working. . . . The class represented by

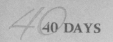

the foolish virgins have been content with a superficial work. They do not know God. . . . Their service . . . degenerates into a form" (*Christ's Object Lessons*, p. 411).

Hence, understanding and experiencing the daily baptism of the Holy Spirit is absolutely essential if one wants to come out of the Laodicean, foolish virgin condition and be among the wise virgins who are ready to meet Jesus when He comes.

Personal Reflection and Discussion

1. Which of the virgins, wise or foolish, are also called Laodicean Christians? _____

_____

_____

2. Which two false attitudes can cause Christians not to be ready for Christ's return? _____

_____

_____

3. What kind of obedience do the foolish virgins have? _____

_____

_____

4. What is the only way foolish virgin Christians can come out of their Laodicean condition? _____

_____

_____

_____

Prayer Activity

● **Call your prayer partner and discuss the devotional with him or her.**
● **Pray with your prayer partner:**
 (1) for God to baptize you with His Holy Spirit
 (2) for God to continue to bring revival in your life and the church
 (3) for God to lead you to come out of the Laodicean condition and become a wise virgin
 (4) for the individuals on your prayer list

Gold, White Raiment, and Eye Salve

In the previous two devotionals we have looked at the foolish virgins of Laodicea and the wise virgins who come out of their Laodicean condition. The wise virgins have the oil, which is the baptism of the Holy Spirit, and Jesus lives in them. The foolish virgins lack these two essential spiritual experiences and therefore their religion is only a hollow form. Their obedience is legalistic and not from the heart. The foolish virgins believe the same doctrines and profess the same hope in Christ's soon return as the wise virgins. However, they are not preparing themselves for that great event.

In Revelation 3 God specifies what is necessary to come out of the Laodicean condition when He instructs the Laodiceans to buy from Him gold, white raiment, and eye salve:

"I counsel thee to buy of me gold tried in the fire, that thou mayest be rich; and white raiment, that thou mayest be clothed, and that the shame of thy nakedness do not appear; and anoint thine eyes with eyesalve, that thou mayest see" (verse 18).

He does this because He loves His children who are in Laodicea and He doesn't want them to be eternally lost.

"As many as I love, I rebuke and chasten: be zealous therefore, and repent" (verse 19).

It is thus essential that Christians today understand and heed God's counsel to the Laodiceans. Our eternal destiny depends on it.

First, God counsels those in Laodicea to "buy" from Him. But we know that eternal life cannot be purchased with the things of this world, such as money:

"Ho, every one that thirsteth, come ye to the waters, and he that hath no money; come ye, buy, and eat; yea, come, buy wine and milk without money and without price" (Isa. 55:1).

"And the Spirit and the bride say, Come. And let him that heareth say, Come. And let him that is athirst come. And whosoever will, let him take the water of life freely" (Rev. 22:17).

No, we do not purchase eternal life with money. Instead, we "buy" from God by giving ourselves to Him completely. We must be willing to let our sinful self and desires be crucified with Christ:

"Knowing this, that our old man is crucified with him, that the body of sin might be destroyed, that henceforth we should not serve sin" (Rom. 6:6).

"Then said Jesus unto his disciples, If any man will come after me, let him deny himself, and take up his cross, and follow me. For whosoever will save his life shall lose it: and whosoever will lose his life for my sake shall find it" (Matt. 16:24, 25).

So what does God want us to "buy" from Him? First, He instructs us to buy "gold," which represents the virtues of faith and love. This gold can be received only by the power of the Holy Spirit fully abiding in us, as illustrated in these verses:

"And hope maketh not ashamed; because the love of God is shed abroad in our hearts by the Holy Ghost which is given unto us" (Rom. 5:5).

"But the fruit of the Spirit is love, joy, peace, longsuffering, gentleness, goodness, faith, meekness, temperance: against such there is no law" (Gal. 5:22, 23).

The white raiment is the justifying and sanctifying righteousness of Christ. It is only as we learn how to let Jesus live out His righteous obedience in us that we

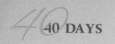

will be clothed in His white raiment. Paul wrote of this to the Galatians:

"I am crucified with Christ: nevertheless I live; yet not I, but Christ liveth in me: and the life which I now live in the flesh I live by the faith of the Son of God, who loved me, and gave himself for me" (Gal. 2:20).

The eye salve is also received only by the Spirit's infilling. It is the Spirit who heals our eyes from their spiritual blindness of our Laodicean condition. It is the Spirit's eye salve that removes the veil that blinds us to the truth of Christ's sanctifying righteousness. If we refuse to receive the baptism of the Holy Spirit, we will continue in our spiritually blind condition and will not grow into the fullness of Christ, which is required to be ready for earth's final events and Christ's return.

Personal Reflection and Discussion

1. What did Jesus mean when He asks us to "buy" from Him? _____

_____

_____

2. What does Jesus counsel the Laodiceans to buy from Him? _____

_____

_____

3. What does the gold, white raiment, and eye salve represent? _____

_____

_____

4. What experience must we have in the Spirit in order to heed Christ's counsel to the Laodiceans?

_____

_____

Prayer Activity

● **Call your prayer partner and discuss the devotional with him or her.**
● **Pray with your prayer partner:**
    (1) for God to baptize you with His Holy Spirit
    (2) for God to continue to bring revival in your life and the church
    (3) for God to lead you to experience the gold, white raiment, and eye salve He offers through the Spirit
    (4) for the individuals on your prayer list

Day 17

Revival and Reformation

Just before Jesus returns there will be two revivals: one false and one true. Jesus warned of false signs and wonders that are so close to the truth that if possible, the "very elect" would be deceived:

"For there shall arise false Christs, and false prophets, and shall shew great signs and wonders; insomuch that, if it were possible, they shall deceive the very elect" (Matt. 24:24).

John the revelator warned that the antichrist would "doeth great wonders, so that he maketh fire come down from heaven on the earth in the sight of men, and deceiveth them that dwell on the earth by the means of those miracles which he had power to do" (Rev. 13:13, 14).

John the Baptist used the symbol of fire to represent the Holy Spirit:

"I indeed baptize you with water unto repentance: but he that cometh after me is mightier than I, whose shoes I am not worthy to bear: he shall baptize you with the Holy Ghost, and with fire" (Matt. 3:11).

Jesus used the same symbolism when He said, "I am come to send fire on the earth; and what will I, if it be already kindled?" (Luke 12:49).

Hence, when the Bible tells us that a power other than God brings down fire, it is referring to a false spirit—a counterfeit spiritual revival. In the verses above we see that counterfeit miracles and wonders will be a big part of the false revival. Revelation tells us further that false revival and miracles will play a major role in deceiving the nations just prior to Christ's return:

"And I saw three unclean spirits like frogs come out of the mouth of the dragon, and out of the mouth of the beast, and out of the mouth of the false prophet. For they are the spirits of devils, working miracles, which go forth unto the kings of the earth and of the whole world, to gather them to the battle of that great day of God Almighty" (Rev. 16:13, 14).

Paul tells us why men and women are deceived by this false revival and counterfeit miracles:

"And with all deceivableness of unrighteousness in them that perish; because they received not the love of the truth, that they might be saved. And for this cause God shall send them strong delusion, that they should believe a lie: that they all might be damned who believed not the truth, but had pleasure in unrighteousness" (2 Thess. 2:10-12).

All who reject the truths of God's Word will be deceived by Satan.

There will also be a great true revival just before Jesus returns. Those who experience this revival from God are those who experience the early and latter rain of the Spirit. The last great outpouring of the Holy Spirit comes in answer to the prayers of God's people. Ellen White described this in the following way:

"When the Third Angel's Message shall go forth with a loud voice, the whole earth shall be lightened with His glory, the Holy Spirit is poured out upon His people. The revenue of glory has been accumulating for this closing work of the Third Angel's Message. The prayers that have been ascending for the fulfillment of the promise, the descent of the Holy Spirit, not one has been lost. Each prayer has been accumulating, ready to overflow and pour forth a healing flood of heavenly influence and accumulated light all over the world" (*Manuscript Releases*, vol. 1, pp. 180, 181).

As a result of growing fully under the early and

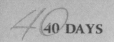

latter rain of the Spirit, God's glory (character) will be seen in the lives of God's people (2 Cor. 3:18). In this manner the earth is lightened with God's glory (Rev. 18:1). A genuine reformation will also be seen in their lives, which will be manifest by obedience to all of God's commandments—an obedience from the heart, because of the Spirit writing God's law on their hearts (2 Cor. 3:3).

Ellen White described this last great reformation that takes place among God's people:

"In visions of the night, representations passed before me of a great reformatory movement among God's people. Many were praising God. The sick were healed, and other miracles were wrought. . . . Hundreds and thousands were seen visiting families and opening before them the word of God. Hearts were convicted by the power of the Holy Spirit, and a spirit of genuine conversion was manifest. On every side doors were thrown open to the proclamation of the truth. The world seemed to be lightened with the heavenly influence. Great blessings were received by the true and humble people of God" (*Testimonies for the Church*, vol. 9, p. 126).

All who are ready to meet Jesus will have experienced this final revival and reformation under the power of the Holy Spirit.

Personal Reflection and Discussion

1. What two revivals will take place just before Jesus returns? _____

_____

_____

2. What characteristics will be seen in the false revival? _____

_____

_____

3. What experience in the Spirit must God's people have in order to experience the last true revival?

_____

_____

4. How does Ellen White describe God's last true revival just before Jesus returns? _____

_____

_____

Prayer Activity

● **Call your prayer partner and discuss the devotional with him or her.**
● **Pray with your prayer partner:**
    (1) for God to baptize you with His Holy Spirit
    (2) for God to continue to bring revival in your life and the church
    (3) for God to shield you from the deceptions of the false revival
    (4) for the individuals on your prayer list

The Shaking of God's Church—Part 1

Just before Jesus returns there will be a great shaking among God's people. The prophet Ezekiel foretold the sealing and shaking:

"He cried also in mine ears with a loud voice, saying, Cause them that have charge over the city to draw near, even every man with his destroying weapon in his hand. And, behold, six men came from the way of the higher gate, which lieth toward the north, and every man a slaughter weapon in his hand; and one man among them was clothed with linen, with a writer's inkhorn by his side: and they went in, and stood beside the brasen altar. And the glory of the God of Israel was gone up from the cherub, whereupon he was, to the threshold of the house. And he called to the man clothed with linen, which had the writer's inkhorn by his side; and the Lord said unto him, Go through the midst of the city, through the midst of Jerusalem, and set a mark upon the foreheads of the men that sigh and that cry for all the abominations that be done in the midst thereof. And to the others he said in mine hearing, Go ye after him through the city, and smite: let not your eye spare, neither have ye pity: slay utterly old and young, both maids, and little children, and women: but come not near any man upon whom is the mark; and begin at my sanctuary. Then they began at the ancient men which were before the house" (Eze. 9:1-6).

In these verses we see that those without the "mark" or seal of God will be "slain," which means shaken out of God's church. Ellen White stated what would cause the shaking:

"I asked the meaning of the shaking I had seen and was shown that it would be caused by the straight testimony called forth by the counsel of the True Witness to the Laodiceans. This will have its effect upon the heart of the receiver, and will lead him to exalt the standard and pour forth the straight truth. Some will not bear this straight testimony. They will rise up against it, and this is what will cause a shaking among God's people" (*Early Writings*, p. 270).

Those who refuse to heed the counsel of the True Witness (Jesus) and let Him fully into their life (Rev. 3:20) through the daily baptism of the Holy Spirit will be shaken out. Remember, the wise virgins have the oil of the Spirit. The foolish virgins do not.

Ellen White gave us a serious warning:

"I then saw the third angel. Said my accompanying angel, 'Fearful is his work. Awful is his mission. He is the angel that is to select the wheat from the tares and seal, or bind, the wheat for the heavenly garner. These things should engross the whole mind, the whole attention'" (*ibid.,* p. 118).

Here we see that the wheat and tares, or the wise and foolish virgins, stay together in the church until the sealing is complete. This references Jesus' parable of the wheat and tares (Matt. 13:24-30). Then the tares or foolish virgins are shaken out from among God's people after the sealing, as Ellen White wrote:

"As soon as God's people are sealed and prepared for the shaking, it will come" (*The Seventh-day Adventist Bible Commentary*, Ellen G. White Comments, vol. 4, p. 1161).

Commenting on Ezekiel 9, Ellen White also wrote:

"The class who do not feel grieved over their own spiritual declension, nor mourn over the sins of others, will be left without the seal of God. The Lord commissions His messengers, the men with slaughtering weapons in their hands: 'Go ye after him through the city, and

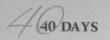

smite: let not your eye spare, neither have ye pity: slay utterly old and young, both maids, and little children, and women: but come not near any man upon whom is the mark; and begin at My sanctuary. Then they began at the ancient men which were before the house.'

"Here we see that the church—the Lord's sanctuary—was the first to feel the stroke of the wrath of God. The ancient men, those to whom God had given great light and who had stood as guardians of the spiritual interests of the people, had betrayed their trust. They had taken the position that we need not look for miracles and the marked manifestation of God's power as in former days. Times have changed. These words strengthen their unbelief, and they say: The Lord will not do good, neither will He do evil. He is too merciful to visit His people in judgment. Thus 'Peace and safety' is the cry from men who will never again lift up their voice like a trumpet to show God's people their transgressions and the house of Jacob their sins. These dumb dogs that would not bark are the ones who feel the just vengeance of an offended God. Men, maidens, and little children all perish together" (*Testimonies for the Church*, vol. 5, p. 211).

It is absolutely necessary for God's people to understand and experience righteousness by faith in order to be sealed:

"Not one of us will ever receive the seal of God while our characters have one spot or stain upon them. It is left with us to remedy the defects in our characters, to cleanse the soul temple of every defilement [righteousness by faith]. Then the latter rain will fall upon us as the early rain fell upon the disciples on the Day of Pentecost" (*ibid.*, p. 214).

The only way one's character will not have a spot or stain is to understand and experience righteousness by faith in Christ alone.

Personal Reflection and Discussion

1. What is the characteristic of those who receive the "mark" or seal of God in Ezekiel's prophecy?

_____

2. According to Ellen White, what causes the shaking in the church? _____

_____

3. Who is the True Witness to the Laodiceans, and what is His message to them? _____

_____

4. What must God's people do to be ready for the shaking experience before it comes? _____

_____

Prayer Activity

● **Call your prayer partner and discuss the devotional with him or her.**
● **Pray with your prayer partner:**
    (1) for God to baptize you with His Holy Spirit
    (2) for God to continue to bring revival in your life and the church
    (3) for God to lead you to receive His seal
    (4) for the individuals on your prayer list

The Shaking of God's Church—Part 2

It will be the Sunday law that completes the sealing and begins the shaking process. Ellen White wrote:

"The Lord has shown me clearly that the image of the beast will be formed before probation closes; for it is to be the great test for the people of God, by which their eternal destiny will be decided. [Rev. 13:11-17 quoted.]

"This is the test that the people of God must have before they are sealed. All who proved their loyalty to God by observing His law, and refusing to accept a spurious sabbath, will rank under the banner of the Lord God Jehovah, and will receive the seal of the living God. Those who yield the truth of heavenly origin and accept the Sunday sabbath will receive the mark of the beast" (*The SDA Bible Commentary*, Ellen G. White Comments, vol. 7, p. 976).

This being the case, if we choose to wait for the institution of the Sunday law to get serious about serving God, it will be too late.

There is a close relationship between the antichrist's false sabbath, righteousness by faith, and the shaking. Ellen White pointed out:

"The time is not far distant when the test will come to every soul. The observance of the false sabbath will be urged upon us. The contest will be between the commandments of God and the commandments of men. Those who have yielded step by step to worldly demands and conformed to worldly customs will then yield to the powers that be, rather than subject themselves to derision, insult, threatened imprisonment, and death. At that time the gold will be separated from the dross. True godliness will be clearly distinguished from the appearance and tinsel of it. Many a star that we have admired for its brilliance will then go out in darkness [shaking].

Those who have assumed the ornaments of the sanctuary, but are not clothed with Christ's righteousness [righteousness by faith], will then appear in the shame of their own nakedness" (*Prophets and Kings*, p. 188).

It is a sad truth, but many of those who have professed faith in Christ and His last warning message will still be shaken out from God's people. They have not let Christ reign fully in their life through the daily baptism of the Holy Spirit. They have not let Christ live out His righteous, obedient life in and through them.

"As the storm approaches, a large class who have professed faith in the third angel's message, but have not been sanctified through obedience to the truth [righteousness by faith], abandon their position and join the ranks of the opposition. By uniting with the world and partaking of its spirit, they have come to view matters in nearly the same light; and when the test is brought, they are prepared to choose the easy, popular side. Men of talent and pleasing address, who once rejoiced in the truth, employ their powers to deceive and mislead souls. They become the most bitter enemies of their former brethren. When Sabbathkeepers are brought before the courts to answer for their faith, these apostates are the most efficient agents of Satan to misrepresent and accuse them, and by false reports and insinuations to stir up the rulers against them" (*The Great Controversy,* p. 608).

Note that it is the third angel who gathers the tares and wheat, and the gathering is done through the final message (Rev. 14:9-12). It is not simply an intellectual message about the Sabbath/Sunday issue, it is a message of righteousness by faith. Only as we experience Jesus living in us, through the baptism of the Holy Spirit and righteousness by faith in Christ alone, will we be faithful

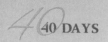

to the end. Regarding this message, Ellen White wrote:

"Several have written to me, inquiring if the message of justification by faith is the third angel's message, and I have answered, 'It is the third angel's message in verity'" (in *Review and Herald*, Apr. 1, 1890).

The logical question would be "What is the relationship between righteousness by faith and the third angel's message?" I will answer by asking another question. What is the *purpose* of the third angel's message? It calls men and women to obey God's commandments, which of course includes the fourth commandment, and gives a warning against receiving the "mark of the beast."

Second, what is the purpose of the message of righteousness by faith in Christ? It leads men and women to obey God's commandments as they, by way of faith, allow Christ to live out His life of righteous obedience to God's law through them. Ellen White wrote of this connection:

"The Lord in His great mercy sent a most precious message to His people through Elders Waggoner and Jones. This message was to bring more prominently before the world the uplifted Saviour, the sacrifice for the sins of the whole world. It presented justification through faith in the Surety; it invited the people to receive the righteousness of Christ, *which is made manifest in obedience to all the commandments of God*" (*Testimonies to Ministers,* pp. 91, 92; italics supplied).

Therefore, one must understand and experience righteousness by faith, which is the third angel's message. It is the sealing message, which protects one from being shaken out from among God's people.

Personal Reflection and Discussion

1. What event prophesied in Revelation 13:15-17 brings about the sealing and shaking of God's people?

_____

2. What will those in the church who have not received the baptism of the Holy Spirit do when Sunday laws begin to be enforced? _____

_____

3. How is the third angel's message, justification, and righteousness by faith related? _____

_____

4. What will happen to us if we wait until the Sunday law is promoted before we get serious about serving God? _____

_____

Prayer Activity

● **Call your prayer partner and discuss the devotional with him or her.**
● **Pray with your prayer partner:**
    (1) for God to baptize you with His Holy Spirit
    (2) for God to continue to bring revival in your life and the church
    (3) for God to lead you to experience Christ to the fullest in your life so you will be ready for Satan's last great deception
    (4) for the individuals on your prayer list

Day 20

The Battle of Armageddon

There is probably no better-known biblical battle than Armageddon. For decades both religious and secular writers have used it to describe a great clash of superpowers that brings worldwide destruction. In truth, the battle of Armageddon describes Satan's effort to destroy God's people, and God's intervention to overthrow his evil forces. The name "Armageddon" refers symbolically to the place where those who are deceived are gathered. Similar symbolism is used for those who accept Christ and are described as coming to Mount Zion and Jerusalem (Heb. 12:22).

Armageddon is described in Revelation 16:

"And I saw three unclean spirits like frogs come out of the mouth of the dragon, and out of the mouth of the beast, and out of the mouth of the false prophet. For they are the spirits of devils, working miracles, which go forth unto the kings of the earth and of the whole world, to gather them to the battle of that great day of God Almighty. Behold, I come as a thief. Blessed is he that watcheth, and keepeth his garments, lest he walk naked, and they see his shame. And he gathered them together into a place called in the Hebrew tongue Armageddon" (verses 13-16).

Ellen White described the gathering work of Satan at this time:

"The present is a solemn fearful time for the church. . . . Satan is also mustering his forces of evil, going forth 'unto the kings of the earth and of the whole world,' to gather them under his banner, to be trained for 'the battle of that great day of God Almighty'" (*The SDA Bible Commentary*, Ellen G. White Comments, vol. 7, p. 983).

Ellen White clearly understood that Satan is already working to gather men and women to his side. Those deceived by him will find themselves fighting against God and His people in the "battle of that great day of God Almighty"—the battle of Armageddon. The gathering and warfare is taking place even now and will culminate when Christ comes to fight for His people and deliver them out of Satan's power (Rev. 19:11-21). This battle will commence again at the end of the 1,000-year period described in Revelation 20, when Satan and his host will attempt to attack God and His people in the New Jerusalem. The result will be the final destruction of Satan and all his followers.

Revelation 16:13, 14 describes Satan's efforts to gather the world and its leaders to his side in his great controversy with Christ. He uses the religious powers of the world to deceive and lead multitudes to his side of the battle against God and His people.

Christ warned His people of Satan's efforts (Matt. 24:24). Sadly, many will still be deceived by Satan's efforts and will actually think they are serving God (Matt. 7:20-23). Christ points out that the real evidence of our relationship with God is the "fruits" of our lives, not miracles and other apparent gifts of the Spirit (verse 20). Many will be deceived because they do not love the truth of God's Word (2 Thess. 2:9-12). God's truth is our only shield against Satan's deceptions (Ps. 91:4).

There are only two groups living on earth when Jesus returns: those who follow God and those who follow Satan. Many contrasts are portrayed in Revelation when comparing those gathered by Christ and those gathered by Satan. Those gathered by Satan stay in Babylon (Rev. 18:4), have the mark or name

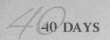

of the beast (Satan's character of lawlessness) in their forehead (Rev. 13:15-17), are defiled by Babylon (Rev. 17:1, 2), and are gathered to Armageddon (Rev. 16:16). Those gathered by Christ are in Jerusalem (Heb. 12:22), have the Father's name (character of loving obedience) in their forehead (Rev. 14:1), are not defiled by Babylon (verse 4), and are on Mount Zion (Heb. 12:22; Rev. 14:1).

Only those "who keep their garment" (see Rev. 16:15)—who experience righteousness by faith in Christ as a sin-pardoning and sin-delivering Savior—will avoid being gathered to Armageddon and be saved. Person-ally experiencing the gospel of righteousness by faith in Christ alone will enable God's people to be able to stand in the day of Christ's return. They will be covered with His garment of righteousness, and no one who has let Him manifest Himself in their life will stand naked in their own self-righteousness. All others will be destroyed.

This can happen to the fullest only when we are filled with God's Spirit. It is the Spirit that writes the law of God in our heart. It is by the Spirit that Christ lives in us and the righteousness of the law is fulfilled in us, causing us to walk in the Spirit and not in the flesh (Rom. 8:4).

Personal Reflection and Discussion

1. What does the battle of Armageddon describe? _____
_____
_____

2. How does Satan gather individuals to his side at Armageddon? _____
_____
_____

3. Who are the two groups of people living on earth when Jesus returns? _____
_____
_____

4. What is meant by "Blessed is he that watcheth, and keepeth his garments, lest he walk naked, and they see his shame" (Rev. 16:15)?_____
_____
_____

Prayer Activity

● **Call your prayer partner and discuss the devotional with him or her.**
● **Pray with your prayer partner:**
> **(1) for God to baptize you with His Holy Spirit**
> **(2) for God to continue to bring revival in your life and the church**
> **(3) for God to enable you to keep Christ's robe of righteous obedience in your life**
> **(4) for the individuals on your prayer list**

Day 21

Miracles

The Bible—notably the words of Jesus Himself— have some very important teachings on miracles. Those who go through earth's final events need to understand the truth about miracles. If not, they will either be deceived or miss out on great blessings.

Some denominations deny that the gifts of the Spirit, which include miracles, healing, prophecy, and tongues (1 Cor. 12:10), belong to the church today. They believe they were only for the apostolic church. Other denominations place such a great emphasis on these kinds of spiritual gifts that they become more susceptible to deception by counterfeit miracles, healings, prophecy, tongues, etc. Then there are denominations that focus so heavily on biblical doctrine with little emphasis on these gifts of the Spirit, even though they believe in spiritual gifts. I have found some Christians in this category to be critical and unaccepting of the more miraculous gifts that occur, fearful that they will be deceived. Then there are those who accept all the gifts of the Spirit, including the more miraculous ones, and even experience them in their own life and ministry. They are balanced in their view and don't seek miracles but let them follow, as Christ said would happen (Mark 16:20).

Jesus performed many miracles and taught that there are genuine miraculous spiritual gifts that will be manifest in the church:

"And these signs shall follow them that believe; In my name shall they cast out devils; they shall speak with new tongues; they shall take up serpents; and if they drink any deadly thing, it shall not hurt them; they shall lay hands on the sick, and they shall recover. So then after the Lord had spoken unto them, he was received up into heaven, and sat on the right hand of God. And they went forth, and preached every where, the Lord working with them, and confirming the word with signs following. Amen" (verses 17-20).

In the book of Acts we read of many miracles such as healing, casting out devils, raising the dead, prophecy, and tongues. In fact, we read that men and women often accepted the gospel message following the manifestation of the gifts of healing (Acts 5:12-16). Hence, miraculous gifts of the Spirit were a part of Jesus' ministry, as well as the ministry of the early church.

Since miracles played an important role in Christ's ministry and the early church, it is understandable that Satan would seek to counterfeit these miraculous gifts in order to deceive. Jesus warned of this also:

"For there shall arise false Christs, and false prophets, and shall shew great signs and wonders; insomuch that, if it were possible, they shall deceive the very elect" (Matt. 24:24).

"Wherefore by their fruits ye shall know them. Not every one that saith unto me, Lord, Lord, shall enter into the kingdom of heaven; but he that doeth the will of my Father which is in heaven. Many will say to me in that day, Lord, Lord, have we not prophesied in thy name? and in thy name have cast out devils? and in thy name done many wonderful works? And then will I profess unto them, I never knew you: depart from me, ye that work iniquity" (Matt. 7:20-23).

The book of Revelation also warns of this type of last-day deception:

"And I saw three unclean spirits like frogs come out of the mouth of the dragon, and out of the mouth of the beast, and out of the mouth of the false prophet. For they are the spirits of devils, working miracles, which

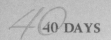

go forth unto the kings of the earth and of the whole world, to gather them to the battle of that great day of God Almighty" (Rev. 16:13, 14).

However, the Christian must not fall into the trap of being suspicious or outright rejecting miracles because of these warnings. It is possible to become more afraid of being deceived by the devil through miracles than to trust the Spirit to lead us into truth. Remember, the context of Christ's statement about blasphemy against the Holy Spirit is when Jewish leaders attributed the work of the Spirit in Jesus to the devil (Matt. 12:24-32). In fact, Ellen White wrote of miracles being a part of God's last work:

"In visions of the night, representations passed before me of a great reformatory movement among God's people. Many were praising God. The sick were healed, and other miracles were wrought. A spirit of intercession was seen, even as was manifested before the great Day of Pentecost" (*Testimonies for the Church*, vol. 9, p. 126).

We have nothing to fear in regard to miracles, and we will be blessed by them if we love Christ and His Word. Those who will be deceived in the last days are those who reject truth:

"And with all deceivableness of unrighteousness in them that perish; because they received not the love of the truth, that they might be saved. And for this cause God shall send them strong delusion, that they should believe a lie: that they all might be damned who believed not the truth, but had pleasure in unrighteousness" (2 Thess. 2:10-12).

Personal Reflection and Discussion

1. What are some attitudes that Christians can have about miracles? _____

_____

2. What did Jesus teach about miracles? What does the book of Revelation teach? _____

_____

3. What is our defense against being deceived by counterfeit miracles? _____

_____

4. What did Ellen White write about miracles and God's last great work? _____

_____

Prayer Activity

● **Call your prayer partner and discuss the devotional with him or her.**
● **Pray with your prayer partner:**
    (1) for God to baptize you with His Holy Spirit
    (2) for God to continue to bring revival in your life and in the church
    (3) for God to lead you to accept all the gifts of the Spirit, including miracles, and shield you from being deceived.
    (4) for the individuals on your prayer list

Day 22

The Antichrist

Several sections of the New Testament refer to the antichrist power. In today's devotional we will focus on just one of these Scriptures. The apostle Paul described the antichrist power in the following way:

"Now we beseech you, brethren, by the coming of our Lord Jesus Christ, and by our gathering together unto him, that ye be not soon shaken in mind, or be troubled, neither by spirit, nor by word, nor by letter as from us, as that the day of Christ is at hand. Let no man deceive you by any means: for that day shall not come, except there come a falling away first, and that man of sin be revealed, the son of perdition; who opposeth and exalteth himself above all that is called God, or that is worshipped; so that he as God sitteth in the temple of God, shewing himself that he is God. Remember ye not, that, when I was yet with you, I told you these things? And now ye know what withholdeth that he might be revealed in his time. For the mystery of iniquity doth already work: only he who now letteth will let, until he be taken out of the way. And then shall that Wicked be revealed, whom the Lord shall consume with the spirit of his mouth, and shall destroy with the brightness of his coming: even him, whose coming is after the working of Satan with all power and signs and lying wonders, and with all deceivableness of unrighteousness in them that perish; because they received not the love of the truth, that they might be saved" (2 Thess. 2:1-10).

Notice several very important teachings in these verses. Paul's statement that this "day shall not come, except there come a falling away first, and that man of sin be revealed, the son of perdition" indicates that the antichrist will arise *before* Christ returns the second time. He is called the "son of perdition," which other transla-tions call "the man of lawlessness" (NIV). Hence, we learn that the antichrist will seek to lead humanity away from obeying God's Ten Commandments. Paul also ex-plains that the antichrist will sit in the "temple of God," which in the New Testament refers to God's church:

"Now therefore ye are no more strangers and for-eigners, but fellowcitizens with the saints, and of the household of God; and are built upon the foundation of the apostles and prophets, Jesus Christ himself being the chief corner stone; in whom all the building fitly framed together groweth unto an holy temple in the Lord: in whom ye also are builded together for an habi-tation of God through the Spirit" (Eph. 2:19-22).

So the antichrist will actually be a religious power who seeks to lead God's people to worship him by turning away from obeying God's law, the Ten Com-mandments.

Paul even gave the timing when this antichrist power will arise:

"For the mystery of iniquity doth already work: only he who now letteth will let, until he be taken out of the way. And then shall that Wicked be revealed" (2 Thess. 2:7, 8).

The word "letteth" actually means to "hold back" (NIV). Early Christians interpreted this verse to mean that the antichrist power would arise after the Roman Empire fell. History reveals that they were correct. The antichrist power reigned over the Holy Roman Empire for centuries once the pagan Roman Empire fell. We also learn from these verses that the antichrist power would reign on earth until Christ's return when he and all who follow him will be destroyed by the "bright-ness of his coming" (verse 8).

53

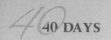

Every Christian today would do well to heed Paul's warning: "And with all deceivableness of unrighteousness in them that perish; because they received not the love of the truth, that they might be saved. And for this cause God shall send them strong delusion, that they should believe a lie: that they all might be damned who believed not the truth, but had pleasure in unrighteousness" (verses 10-12).

Those who do not love and believe the truth of God's Word will be led into the antichrist's deception, resulting in their eternal loss. Here is a clear call to receive the infilling baptism of the Spirit daily because "the love of God is shed abroad in our hearts by the Holy Ghost which is given unto us" (Rom. 5:5), which is the Spirit of truth to lead God's people into the truths of God's Word. The love of God and His truth become deeply rooted in our hearts by the Holy Spirit. Remember, this is why the foolish virgins are lost. They do not have the extra oil, which is the baptism of the Holy Spirit.

Personal Reflection and Discussion

1. Will the antichrist appear before or after Christ's second coming? _____
_____

2. What will he try to cause God's people, as well as everyone in the world, to do? _____
_____

3. Where is the antichrist described as sitting and what does that mean? _____
_____

4. At what time in history will the antichrist arise and begin his work of leading people away from God?
_____

5. How long will the antichrist reign in power? _____
_____

6. Why is it important for Christians to be baptized of the Holy Spirit? _____
_____

Prayer Activity

● **Call your prayer partner and discuss the devotional with him or her.**
● **Pray with your prayer partner:**
    (1) for God to baptize you with His Holy Spirit
    (2) for God to continue to bring revival in your life and the church
    (3) for God to put in your heart the desire to study the Bible and follow it
    (4) for the individuals on your prayer list

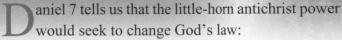

Day 23

The Mark of the Beast

Daniel 7 tells us that the little-horn antichrist power would seek to change God's law:

"And he shall speak great words against the most High, and shall wear out the saints of the most High, and think to change times and laws: and they shall be given into his hand until a time and times and the dividing of time" (Dan. 7:25).

This power changed God's fourth commandment, which reminds us to keep holy God's seventh-day Sabbath (Saturday). Hence, the antichrist power changed God's fourth commandment in order to require worship on Sunday instead of the seventh-day Sabbath. In yesterday's study we saw Paul's warning that the antichrist would seek to lead God's people away from obeying God's law (2 Thess. 2:3, 4).

The Reformation founder of the Lutheran Church, Martin Luther, observed this issue when he wrote:

"They [the dominant church in his day] allege the Sabbath changed into Sunday, the Lord's day, contrary to the Decalogue [Ten Commandments], as it appears; neither is there any example more boasted of than the changing of the Sabbath day. Great, say they, is the power and authority of the church, since it dispensed with one of the Ten Commandments" (Augsburg Confession of Faith, Article 28).

Revelation 13 tells us that this same power will try to force this change onto everyone. Verse 16 tells us that the "mark of the beast" will be enforced, requiring all to receive it either in their hand or forehead in order to buy and sell. All who refuse to receive the mark of the beast will be placed in dire economic circumstances and ultimately condemned to death (verse 15).

Therefore it should be very clear what the "mark"

of the beast's authority is. The antichrist power, by its own authority, boasts of their change of the day of worship from the seventh-day Sabbath to Sunday as their "mark" of authority. Hence, it is clear that the "mark of the beast" is Sunday observance, which is based on the authority of human beings and not God.

On the other hand, obeying the seventh-day Sabbath, as commanded in the fourth commandment of the Decalogue, is based on the authority of God. Just before Jesus returns, Sunday observance will be forced on everyone. All who refuse to receive the mark in their "forehead" by believing the deception, or even simply receiving the mark in their "hand" by observing it—even if they don't believe it—will be severely persecuted. In time they will not be able to "buy or sell," and will ultimately face a death decree for refusing to yield their loyalty to God.

God is very clear in His Word about the importance of the seventh-day Sabbath. Not only does He command it in the fourth commandment (Ex. 20:8-11), He declares it to be a sign between Him and His people that He is their God—the God who sanctifies them (Eze. 20:12, 20). Therefore, to willfully choose to obey Sunday while knowing the seventh-day Sabbath is God's holy day is to worship the beast power, not God. We worship who we obey.

Hence, the last issue in earth's final events centers on whom we choose to worship. Of course, this has always been the issue. Satan has always wanted to receive the worship that only God deserves (Isa. 14:12-14); he even tried to tempt Christ to worship him (Matt. 4:8, 9). Revelation warns us that as part of earth's final events, Satan will lead all the world to

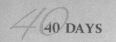

turn from the true God in their worship and to worship him by receiving his mark of the beast. Satan is the influencing power behind the little horn, the antichrist power who seeks to "change times and laws" (Dan. 7:25).

However, God's people have nothing to fear concerning these issues. As they choose to remain faithful to God, He will deliver them from Satan's power.

Some will become martyrs during the "little time of trouble" (Ellen G. White, *Last Day Events*, p. 143). Then, during the "time of trouble," or "tribulation," God will fight for His people by pouring out the seven last plagues, from which His people will be protected (Ps. 91). The plagues will fall on those who received the mark of the beast; those who have chosen to worship the antichrist and not God (Rev. 16).

Personal Reflection and Discussion

1. What did Daniel say the little-horn antichrist power would try to do with God's law? _____

_____

2. What was one of the Ten Commandments the antichrist tried to change? _____

_____

3. What does it mean to receive the mark of the beast in the forehead or hand? _____

_____

4. How does the antichrist try to pressure everyone to receive the mark of the beast? _____

_____

5. What does God call the Sabbath in Ezekiel 20:12, 20? _____

_____

6. Why is obeying Sunday rather than Sabbath (Saturday) so important? _____

_____

Prayer Activity

● **Call your prayer partner and discuss the devotional with him or her.**
● **Pray with your prayer partner:**
    (1) for God to baptize you with His Holy Spirit
    (2) for God to continue to bring revival in your life and the church
    (3) for God to place on your heart the desire to be faithful in obeying Him
    (4) for the individuals on your prayer list

Day 24

The Loud Cry and Little Time of Trouble

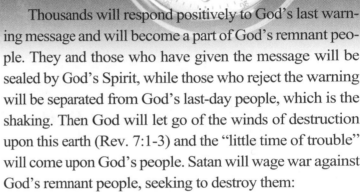

God's last warning to the world is found in Revelation 14:9-12, the third angel's message. Jesus Himself said that the gospel of a sin-pardoning and sin-delivering Savior would be preached in all the world just before the end (Matt. 24:14). Hence, the third angel's message and the gospel message of righteousness by faith are to be proclaimed together just before Jesus comes—a message of justification and sanctification associated with a warning against receiving the mark of the beast.

Through the message of the third angel and righteousness by faith, the earth will be lightened with the glory (character) of Christ (Rev. 18:1).

Revelation 18:2-4 is a warning to be given to all Christians at this time:

"And he cried mightily with a strong voice, saying, Babylon the great is fallen, is fallen, and is become the habitation of devils, and the hold of every foul spirit, and a cage of every unclean and hateful bird. For all nations have drunk of the wine of the wrath of her fornication, and the kings of the earth have committed fornication with her, and the merchants of the earth are waxed rich through the abundance of her delicacies. And I heard another voice from heaven, saying, Come out of her, my people, that ye be not partakers of her sins, and that ye receive not of her plagues."

This is a call to come out of the false churches in order to avoid the seven last plagues. This message will be given under the latter rain power of the Spirit.

God's remnant church is the eyes of the body of Christ. She has the prophetic eye (message) to enlighten God's people in all the churches concerning Satan's last deceptions. She is to present the Sabbath/Sunday issue in clear and distinct lines so everyone will have opportunity to understand the mark-of-the-beast controversy.

Thousands will respond positively to God's last warning message and will become a part of God's remnant people. They and those who have given the message will be sealed by God's Spirit, while those who reject the warning will be separated from God's last-day people, which is the shaking. Then God will let go of the winds of destruction upon this earth (Rev. 7:1-3) and the "little time of trouble" will come upon God's people. Satan will wage war against God's remnant people, seeking to destroy them:

"And the dragon was wroth with the woman, and went to make war with the remnant of her seed, which keep the commandments of God, and have the testimony of Jesus Christ" (Rev. 12:17).

Ellen White described this troubled time:

"Just before we entered it [the time of trouble], we all received the seal of the living God. Then I saw the four angels cease to hold the four winds. And I saw famine, pestilence and sword, nation rose against nation, and the whole world was in confusion" (*The SDA Bible Commentary*, Ellen G. White Comments, vol. 7, p. 968).

Because of the terrible events that will be happening in the world, Sunday laws will be promoted, with many Christians thinking that will keep God's wrath from falling on the earth. Many will say it is because of people desecrating Sunday sacredness that God is angry and pouring out His judgments. Ellen White described the coming judgments and the nominal Christian world's reaction to them:

"The great deceiver will persuade men that those who serve God are causing these evils. . . . It will be declared that men are offending God by the violation of the Sunday sabbath; that this sin has brought calamities which will not cease until Sunday observance shall be strictly enforced; and that those who present

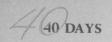

the claims of the fourth commandment, thus destroying reverence for Sunday, are troublers of the people, preventing their restoration to divine favor and temporal prosperity" (*The Great Controversy*, p. 590).

During the "little time of trouble," God's remnant people will be severely persecuted:

"As the defenders of truth refuse to honor the Sunday-sabbath, some of them will be thrust into prison, some will be exiled, some will be treated as slaves. To human wisdom all this now seems impossible; but as the restraining Spirit of God shall be withdrawn from men, and they shall be under the control of Satan, who hates the divine precepts, there will be strange developments.

The heart can be very cruel when God's fear and love are removed" (*ibid.*, p. 608).

All this may sound like a very fearful time. However, God's people have nothing to fear. Through the daily baptism of the Holy Spirit and by experiencing righteousness by faith in Christ alone, Jesus will be living in His people, strengthening and empowering them to be faithful to Him.

At the end of this "little time of trouble," the judgment will end and the "time of trouble" or "tribulation" will commence. At that time, every case for eternity will have been decided; everyone will remain saved or lost (Rev. 22:11). Because God is no longer offering mercy to the unrepentant at that time, none of God's people will be martyred.

Personal Reflection and Discussion

1. God will use the proclamation of the gospel through a message of _____ and _____, and the warning against receiving the _____ of the beast to call the world to obedience to Himself.

2. During the "little time of trouble," what does God call His people to come out of? _____
_____

3. What disastrous events are happening in the world during the "little time of trouble"? _____
_____

4. Who does the world blame for these terrible events and why? _____
_____

5. What does Satan lead the world to do to God's people? _____
_____

6. Why should God's people not be afraid of this "little time of trouble"? _____
_____

Prayer Activity

● **Call your prayer partner and discuss the devotional with him or her.**
● **Pray with your prayer partner:**
    (1) for God to baptize you with His Holy Spirit
    (2) for God to continue to bring revival in your life and the church
    (3) for God to do in your life whatever is necessary to prepare you to be faithful to Him during the "little time of trouble"
    (4) for the individuals on your prayer list

Day 25

Living Without Christ as Mediator

Those living when Jesus returns will be living during a time in history very different from any other time since the fall of Adam. Ever since the fall of humanity, God's mercy has been seen and felt in this world. God has many times intervened to hold back Satan's destructive efforts. Even now the angels are holding back the destructive forces of this earth until God's children are sealed by the Holy Spirit (Rev. 7:1-3; Eph. 4:30).

However, after the judgment has ended and all cases of humanity's destiny will have been decided, human beings will be living without Christ as mediator in the heavenly sanctuary.

"And the temple was filled with smoke from the glory of God, and from his power; and no man was able to enter into the temple, till the seven plagues of the seven angels were fulfilled" (Rev. 15:8).

Those who have chosen to follow Christ will remain faithful and those who have chosen Satan as their leader will stay in his camp.

"He that is unjust, let him be unjust still: and he which is filthy, let him be filthy still: and he that is righteous, let him be righteous still: and he that is holy, let him be holy still. And, behold, I come quickly; and my reward is with me, to give every man according as his work shall be" (Rev. 22:11, 12).

During that time the seven last plagues will fall on the wicked without any of God's mercy mingled with this judgment (Rev. 15:6, 8; 16:1; 14:9, 10).

Since Christ is no longer mediating as high priest, God's people will need to have attained a condition of complete victory over all sin in their lives. They will be living in no known sin. They will not be sinning in thought, word, or deed. They can live in victory because

Christ is fully manifesting Himself in and through their lives. In relation to this topic Ellen White wrote:

"'The prince of this world cometh,' said Jesus, 'and hath nothing in Me.' John 14:30. There was in Him nothing that responded to Satan's sophistry. He did not consent to sin. Not even by a thought did He yield to temptation. So it may be with us" (*The Desire of Ages*, p. 123).

"Those who are living upon the earth when the intercession of Christ shall cease in the sanctuary above are to stand in the sight of a holy God without a mediator. Their robes must be spotless, their characters must be purified from sin by the blood of sprinkling" (*The Great Controversy*, p. 425).

This must be the experience of those who are ready to meet Jesus, since they will no longer have the mediatory intercession of Christ to turn to if they sin in thought, word, or deed. That may sound like an impossibility—yet it is true. Ellen White describes God's people who are living at that time as follows:

"In the time of trouble, if the people of God had unconfessed sins to appear before them while tortured with fear and anguish, they would be overwhelmed; despair would cut off their faith, and they could not have confidence to plead with God for deliverance. But while they have a deep sense of their unworthiness, they have no concealed wrongs to reveal. Their sins have gone beforehand to judgment and have been blotted out, and they cannot bring them to remembrance" (*ibid.*, p. 620).

Jude refers to the experience of that last generation of Christians who are living when Jesus comes:

"Now unto him that is able to keep you from fall-

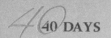

ing, and to present you faultless before the presence of his glory with exceeding joy" (Jude 24).

Jude explains that those who allow Christ to "keep them from falling" into sin will stand in the "presence of his glory with exceeding joy" when He returns. Those filled with the Holy Spirit will not be consumed. Jesus described His second coming, which is the same Greek word used in Jude 24 for "glory," in Matthew 24:30: "And then shall appear the sign of the Son of man in heaven: and then shall all the tribes of the earth mourn, and they shall see the Son of man coming in the clouds of heaven with power and great glory."

In contrast, those who have not experienced the purifying power of God will be killed by the "brightness of His coming" (2 Thess. 2:8).

Jude also says that the Lord will present His people "faultless" when they stand in the presence of His glory. This is the same Greek word used to describe that last generation of Christians who give the three angels' messages in power just before Jesus comes:

"And in their mouth was found no guile: for they are without fault before the throne of God" (Rev. 14:5).

This amazing experience can take place in the Christian's life only as the baptism of the Holy Spirit and Christ's justifying and sanctifying righteousness are understood and experienced.

Personal Reflection and Discussion

1. How is the time just before Jesus returns different than any other time in the history of this world?

_____

2. How does Ellen White describe God's people who are living when Christ ends His mediatory work in the heavenly sanctuary? _____

_____

3. How can God's people have confidence during the "little time of trouble" to plead with God for deliverance from Satan's persecuting power? _____

_____

4. How do Jude 24 and Revelation 14:5 describe God's last-day people? _____

_____

5. What three things must God's last-day people understand and experience? _____

_____

Prayer Activity

● Call your prayer partner and discuss the devotional with him or her.
● Pray with your prayer partner:
    (1) for God to baptize you with His Holy Spirit
    (2) for God to continue to bring revival in your life and the church
    (3) for God to lead you to understand and experience Christ's justifying and sanctifying righteousness
    (4) for the individuals on your prayer list

Day 26

The Time of Trouble or Tribulation

The time of trouble or tribulation will soon come upon this earth. The angels of Revelation 7 are about to let go of the winds of destruction. Daniel described the event:

"At that time shall Michael stand up, the great Prince which standeth for the children of thy people: and there shall be a time of trouble, such as never was since there was a nation even to that same time: and at that time thy people shall be delivered, every one that shall be found written in the book" (Dan. 12:1).

Ellen White described this serious time in the following way:

"When the third angel's message closes, mercy no longer pleads for the guilty inhabitants of the earth. The people of God have accomplished their work. They have received 'the latter rain,' 'the refreshing from the presence of the Lord,' and they are prepared for the trying hour before them. Angels are hastening to and fro in heaven. An angel returning from the earth announces that his work is done; the final test has been brought upon the world, and all who have proved themselves loyal to the divine precepts have received 'the seal of the living God.' Then Jesus ceases His intercession in the sanctuary above. He lifts His hands and with a loud voice says, 'It is done;' and all the angelic host lay off their crowns as He makes the solemn announcement: 'He that is unjust, let him be unjust still: and he which is filthy, let him be filthy still: and he that is righteous, let him be righteous still: and he that is holy, let him be holy still.' Revelation 22:11. Every case has been decided for life or death. Christ has made the atonement for His people and blotted out their sins. The number of His subjects is made up; 'the kingdom and dominion, and the greatness of the kingdom under the whole heaven,' is about to be given to the heirs of salvation, and Jesus is to reign as King of kings and Lord of lords.

"When He leaves the sanctuary, darkness covers the inhabitants of the earth. In that fearful time the righteous must live in the sight of a holy God without an intercessor. The restraint which has been upon the wicked is removed, and Satan has entire control of the finally impenitent. God's long-suffering has ended. The world has rejected His mercy, despised His love, and trampled upon His law. The wicked have passed the boundary of their probation; the Spirit of God, persistently resisted, has been at last withdrawn. Unsheltered by divine grace, they have no protection from the wicked one. Satan will then plunge the inhabitants of the earth into one great, final trouble. As the angels of God cease to hold in check the fierce winds of human passion, all the elements of strife will be let loose. The whole world will be involved in ruin more terrible than that which came upon Jerusalem of old" (*The Great Controversy*, pp. 613, 614).

For God's people, the time of trouble will be a time of severe testing of their faith. All the forces of earth and hell will be against them. To the natural eye, the future looks very foreboding. All God's people will have to cling to the promises of God's Word. The lessons they have learned through trusting God during the difficult times in their lives will be a great blessing at this time. However, their greatest concern is if every sin has been confessed and if they have faithfully represented their Savior.

Satan's desire is to destroy God's people during

61

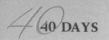

the time of trouble. However, instead of destroying God's people, the time of trouble will actually continue the work of purifying them in preparation for Christ's glorious return. Ellen White described this purification process:

"While Satan seeks to destroy this class, God will send His angels to comfort and protect them in the time of peril. The assaults of Satan are fierce and determined, his delusions are terrible; but the Lord's eye is upon His people, and His ear listens to their cries. Their affliction is great, the flames of the furnace seem about to consume them; but the Refiner will bring them forth as gold tried in the fire. God's love for His children during the period of their severest trial is as strong and tender as in the days of their sunniest prosperity; but it is needful for them to be placed in the furnace of fire; their earthliness must be consumed, that the image of Christ may be perfectly reflected" (*ibid*, p. 621).

We are living in serious times. Every Christian must wake up to the fact that Christ is about to return. The earth is about to experience the most terrible times in its history. We must take our relationship with Christ very seriously and let Him lead us into victory over sin through faith in His righteousness.

Personal Reflection and Discussion

1. When does the time of trouble begin? _____

_____

2. What will have been the experience of God's people just before the time of trouble begins? _____

_____

3. What will be the primary concern of God's people during the time of trouble? _____

_____

4. Why will God allow His people to go through the time of trouble? _____

_____

5. What kind of relationship must we have in order to be faithful to God during the time of trouble?

_____

_____

Prayer Activity

- **Call your prayer partner and discuss the devotional with him or her.**
- **Pray with your prayer partner:**
    - **(1) for God to baptize you with His Holy Spirit**
    - **(2) for God to continue to bring revival in your life and the church**
    - **(3) for God to lead you into a strong, meaningful relationship with Christ so you will be faithful to God during the time of trouble**
    - **(4) for the individuals on your prayer list**

Day 27

The Seven Last Plagues

Revelation 16 describes seven terrible plagues that will fall on those who have received the mark of the beast. They begin occurring when the investigative judgment is complete (Rev. 15:8). The work in the temple in heaven is finished. Every case is decided for eternity, and Jesus is soon to return to earth (Rev. 22:11, 12). Therefore, the plagues take place during the "time of trouble" or "tribulation" (Dan. 12:1).

The first four plagues fall one after the other in various parts of the world (Rev. 16:1). These plagues are (1) terrible sores, (2) sea becomes as blood, (3) fresh waters become as blood, and (4) the sun scorches the earth (Rev. 16:2-9). The last three plagues fall very close together, and they are closely connected with Christ's second coming.

The fifth plague fills the kingdom of the beast with darkness, which is the entire world at that time. This is the first time the unrepentant realize they are lost. They sense their spiritual darkness, but it is too late (verses 10, 11).

The sixth plague is poured upon the river Euphrates and it dries up, which prepares the way for the kings of the east (verse 12). The Euphrates' waters represent the people who support spiritual Babylon (Rev. 17:15). Spiritual Babylon is pictured as sitting on "many waters" (verse 1), which would be the spiritual river Euphrates, using the imagery of Old Testament Babylon. Literal Babylon was also situated on the Euphrates River (Jer. 51:12, 13, 63, 64).

We can learn much about the meaning of the sixth plague's imagery by understanding how literal Old Testament Babylon fell. Babylon was situated over the river Euphrates. Cyrus, the Medo-Persian king, conquered Babylon in one night by drying up the riverbed and marching his armies into the city on dry ground. God had predicted this centuries before it happened, even naming Cyrus and calling him the anointed (Isa. 45:1). In this same manner, the sixth plague describes the rapid fall of spiritual Babylon. Her spiritual waters—her underlying support—is dried up. This prepares the way for the kings of the east—Christ and His angels—who are pictured as coming from the east (Matt. 24:27).

At the seventh plague the voice of God is heard, a mighty earthquake rocks the world, and great hailstones fall (Rev. 16:17-21). This is the moment Christ appears to deliver His people.

In some ways God is fighting for His people during the tribulation through pouring out the seven last plagues. The plagues then culminate with Christ's return to deliver His people from the murderous rage of those deceived by Satan.

God's people have nothing to fear from the plagues. They are called the "wrath of God" (Rev. 16:1), and Christ has already suffered God's wrath on the cross for His people. All who accept Christ escape God's wrath, which will be exhibited in the plagues, because the blood of Christ covers them. This is similar to the Passover experience of Israel in Egypt when the destroying angel passed over the homes of all who had the blood on the doorpost and did not destroy the firstborn of that home.

God's promise in Psalm 91 is a wonderful reassurance to God's people during the plagues:

"He that dwelleth in the secret place of the most High shall abide under the shadow of the Almighty. I will say of the Lord, He is my refuge and my fortress: my God; in him will I trust. Surely he shall deliver thee

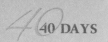

from the snare of the fowler, and from the noisome pestilence. He shall cover thee with his feathers, and under his wings shalt thou trust: his truth shall be thy shield and buckler. Thou shalt not be afraid for the terror by night; nor for the arrow that flieth by day; nor for the pestilence that walketh in darkness; nor for the destruction that wasteth at noonday. A thousand shall fall at thy side, and ten thousand at thy right hand; but it shall not come nigh thee. Only with thine eyes shalt thou behold and see the reward of the wicked. Because thou hast made the Lord, which is my refuge, even the most High, thy habitation; there shall no evil befall thee, neither shall any plague come nigh thy dwelling. For he shall give his angels charge over thee, to keep thee in all thy ways" (verses 1-11).

Personal Reflection and Discussion

1. Upon whom do the seven last plagues fall? _____

_____

2. Why do the righteous stay righteous and the unrighteous stay unrighteous during the seven last plagues? _____

_____

3. List the first four plagues:

_____

_____

4. List the last three plagues:

_____

_____

5. Why do God's people need not fear the seven last plagues? _____

_____

Prayer Activity

● **Call your prayer partner and discuss the devotional with him or her.**
● **Pray with your prayer partner:**
    (1) for God to baptize you with His Holy Spirit
    (2) for God to continue to bring revival in your life and the church
    (3) for God to lead you to have the relationship with Christ you must have in order to avoid receiving the seven last plagues
    (4) for the individuals on your prayer list

1,000 Years of Peace

Revelation 20 describes a 1,000-year period when Satan and his evil angels will be bound and unable to deceive anyone:

"And I saw an angel come down from heaven, having the key of the bottomless pit and a great chain in his hand. and he laid hold on the dragon, that old serpent, which is the Devil, and Satan, and bound him a thousand years, and cast him into the bottomless pit, and shut him up, and set a seal upon him, that he should deceive the nations no more, till the thousand years should be fulfilled: and after that he must be loosed a little season" (verses 1-3).

The "great chain" is a chain of circumstances that keep Satan from deceiving anyone for 1,000 years. Why is this the case? First, the 1,000-year period begins with the second coming of Christ, the time in which all His people will be caught up to meet Him in the air. They will then return to heaven with Jesus for 1,000 years.

"For the Lord himself shall descend from heaven with a shout, with the voice of the archangel, and with the trump of God: and the dead in Christ shall rise first: then we which are alive and remain shall be caught up together with them in the clouds, to meet the Lord in the air: and so shall we ever be with the Lord" (1 Thess. 4:16, 17).

These texts continue to provide a glimpse of heaven:

"And I saw thrones, and they sat upon them, and judgment was given unto them: and I saw the souls of them that were beheaded for the witness of Jesus, and for the word of God, and which had not worshipped the beast, neither his image, neither had received his mark upon their foreheads, or in their hands; and they lived and reigned with Christ a thousand years" (Rev. 20:4).

"Blessed and holy is he that hath part in the first resurrection: on such the second death hath no power,

but they shall be priests of God and of Christ, and shall reign with him a thousand years" (verse 6).

The unrighteous, on the other hand, will "be revealed, whom the Lord shall consume with the spirit of his mouth, and shall destroy with the brightness of his coming" (2 Thess. 2:8). Hence, Satan is described as being chained in a bottomless pit because he has no one to deceive since the righteous are in heaven and the unrighteous wicked are dead.

During the 1,000 years the earth is in a dark, desolate condition, which will be the dwelling place of Satan and his evil angels. Jeremiah described the earth during that time in the following way:

"I beheld the earth, and, lo, it was without form, and void; and the heavens, and they had no light. I beheld the mountains, and, lo, they trembled, and all the hills moved lightly. I beheld, and, lo, there was no man, and all the birds of the heavens were fled. I beheld, and, lo, the fruitful place was a wilderness, and all the cities thereof were broken down at the presence of the Lord, and by his fierce anger. For thus hath the Lord said, The whole land shall be desolate; yet will I not make a full end" (Jer. 4:23-27).

At the end of the 1,000 years Jesus returns to earth with His people and the New Jerusalem:

"And I John saw the holy city, new Jerusalem, coming down from God out of heaven, prepared as a bride adorned for her husband" (Rev. 21:2).

At that time all the unrighteous in their graves will be resurrected: " But the rest of the dead lived not again until the thousand years were finished" (Rev. 20:5).

The Bible tells us that Satan won't have changed during the 1,000 years; he will still hate God. So when the unrighteous are resurrected, he deceives them into

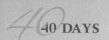

thinking they can attack and overcome the New Jerusalem, where Christ and the saints are:

"And when the thousand years are expired, Satan shall be loosed out of his prison, and shall go out to deceive the nations which are in the four quarters of the earth, Gog and Magog, to gather them together to battle: the number of whom is as the sand of the sea. And they went up on the breadth of the earth, and compassed the camp of the saints about, and the beloved city: and fire came down from God out of heaven, and devoured them" (verses 7-9).

Shortly after the attack on the Holy City, New Jerusalem, God executes His judgment against them and they are destroyed by fire. God is fair and gives them opportunity to realize why they are lost, which is described as the "great white throne" judgment right before they receive God's just penalty of eternal death for their sins (verse 11).

"Then shall he say also unto them on the left hand, Depart from me, ye cursed, into everlasting fire, prepared for the devil and his angels" (Matt. 25:41).

The believer in Jesus Christ has nothing to fear. As the Lamb of God, Jesus received the wrath of God on behalf of His people. Only those without Christ's blood covering them will experience the second death in the lake of fire.

Personal Reflection and Discussion

1. What event begins the 1,000 years? _____

2. What happens to God's people at the beginning of the 1,000 years, and where do they spend the 1,000 years? _____

3. What happens to the followers of Satan at the beginning of the 1,000 years? _____

4. Why is Satan unable to deceive anyone during the 1,000 years? _____

5. Who and what comes to this earth at the end of the 1,000 years? _____

6. What does Satan do at the end of the 1,000 years? _____

7. What happens to Satan and his followers at the end of the 1,000 years? _____

Prayer Activity

● Call your prayer partner and discuss the devotional with him or her.
● Pray with your prayer partner:
    (1) for God to baptize you with His Holy Spirit
    (2) for God to continue to bring revival in your life and the church
    (3) for God to prepare you to go to heaven with Jesus during the 1,000 years
    (4) for the individuals on your prayer list

Day 29

The Great White Throne Judgment

Lucifer was created as a wise and beautiful angel. However, he was not satisfied with his position. The prophet Ezekiel described Lucifer's original position in heaven using the symbol of the king of Tyrus:

"Son of man, take up a lamentation upon the king of Tyrus, and say unto him, Thus saith the Lord God; Thou sealest up the sum, full of wisdom, and perfect in beauty. . . . Thou art the anointed cherub that covereth; and I have set thee so: thou wast upon the holy mountain of God; thou hast walked up and down in the midst of the stones of fire. Thou wast perfect in thy ways from the day that thou wast created, till iniquity was found in thee. . . . Thou hast sinned: therefore I will cast thee as profane out of the mountain of God: and I will destroy thee, O covering cherub, from the midst of the stones of fire. Thine heart was lifted up because of thy beauty, thou hast corrupted thy wisdom by reason of thy brightness" (Eze. 28:12-17).

Lucifer's pride led him to desire to be exalted to God's position and be worshipped by all of creation:

"How art thou fallen from heaven, O Lucifer, son of the morning! how art thou cut down to the ground, which didst weaken the nations! For thou hast said in thine heart, I will ascend into heaven, I will exalt my throne above the stars of God: I will sit also upon the mount of the congregation, in the sides of the north: I will ascend above the heights of the clouds; I will be like the most High" (Isa. 14:12-14).

We see this desire to be worshipped in his last temptation of Christ in the wilderness:

"Again, the devil taketh him up into an exceeding high mountain, and sheweth him all the kingdoms of the world, and the glory of them; and saith unto him, All these things will I give thee, if thou wilt fall down and worship me" (Matt. 4:8, 9).

This desire of Satan's to be worshipped as God led to conflict in heaven between the angels who followed him and those who remained faithful to God:

"And there was war in heaven: Michael and his angels fought against the dragon; and the dragon fought and his angels, and prevailed not; neither was their place found any more in heaven. And the great dragon was cast out, that old serpent, called the Devil, and Satan, which deceiveth the whole world: he was cast out into the earth, and his angels were cast out with him" (Rev. 12:7-9).

The same spirit of pride and rebellion is in the heart of sinful man: "The carnal mind is enmity against God: for it is not subject to the law of God, neither indeed can be" (Rom. 8:7).

This is why at the end of the 1,000 years of Revelation 20, the resurrected followers of Satan still have rebellion in their hearts and try to attack the New Jerusalem. Just before they are eternally lost, they will face what is called the "great white throne" judgment:

"And I saw a great white throne, and him that sat on it, from whose face the earth and the heaven fled away; and there was found no place for them. And I saw the dead, small and great, stand before God; and the books were opened: and another book was opened, which is the book of life: and the dead were judged out of those things which were written in the books, according to their works. And the sea gave up the dead which were in it; and death and hell delivered up the dead which were in them: and they were judged every man according to their works" (Rev. 20:11-13).

When this "great white throne" judgment takes

67

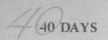

place, every lost soul will clearly see their life of rebellion and why they are lost. As they stand before God's judgment throne they must face their life of sin and their rejection of God's offer of salvation through Christ. As the result of this powerful revelation of God and their unrighteousness, they bow before Him, acknowledging His just condemnation of their rebellion and sin:

"For it is written, As I live, saith the Lord, every knee shall bow to me, and every tongue shall confess to God. So then every one of us shall give account of himself to God" (Rom. 14:11, 12).

Once Satan, his host of evil angels, and all lost sinners acknowledge God's righteous judgment, their final destruction will take place:

"And death and hell were cast into the lake of fire. This is the second death. And whosoever was not found written in the book of life was cast into the lake of fire" (Rev. 20:14, 15).

As we have seen in this devotional, "We then, as workers together with him, beseech you also that ye receive not the grace of God in vain. (For he saith, I have heard thee in a time accepted, and in the day of salvation have I succoured thee: behold, now is the accepted time; behold, now is the day of salvation.)" (2 Cor. 6:1, 2).

Of those who refuse to heed God's appeal, God said through Zechariah:

"But they refused to hearken, and pulled away the shoulder, and stopped their ears, that they should not hear. Yea, they made their hearts as an adamant stone, lest they should hear the law, and the words which the Lord of hosts hath sent in his spirit by the former prophets: therefore came a great wrath from the Lord of hosts. Therefore it is come to pass, that as he cried, and they would not hear; so they cried, and I would not hear, saith the Lord of hosts" (Zech. 7:11-13).

Personal Reflection and Discussion

1. What attitude of Satan led to His rebellion against God? _____

2. What attitude does Satan want everyone to have toward him? _____

3. What is the last great judgment called in the book of Revelation? _____
_____

4. What do those who have rejected Christ do as a result of this judgment? _____
_____

5. What happens to those who have rejected Christ when the "great white throne" judgment is complete?
_____

Prayer Activity

- Call your prayer partner and discuss the devotional with him or her.
- Pray with your prayer partner:
    (1) for God to baptize you with His Holy Spirit
    (2) for God to continue to bring revival in your life and the church
    (3) to thank God for the peace you have about the "great white throne" judgment.
    (4) for the individuals on your prayer list

Day 30

The New Earth

Jesus said, "Blessed are the meek: for they shall inherit the earth" (Matt. 5:5). The earth Jesus spoke of in this verse is not the present world of sin. As we studied yesterday, at the end of the 1,000 years, Satan, the evil angels, and all the unrighteous will be destroyed in the lake of fire (Rev. 20:15). That fire not only burns up Satan and all who rejected Christ's offer of salvation, it also burns up the present world, leaving no trace of sin:

"But the day of the Lord will come as a thief in the night; in the which the heavens shall pass away with a great noise, and the elements shall melt with fervent heat, the earth also and the works that are therein shall be burned up. Seeing then that all these things shall be dissolved, what manner of persons ought ye to be in all holy conversation and godliness, Looking for and hasting unto the coming of the day of God, wherein the heavens being on fire shall be dissolved, and the elements shall melt with fervent heat? Nevertheless we, according to his promise, look for new heavens and a new earth, wherein dwelleth righteousness. Wherefore, beloved, seeing that ye look for such things, be diligent that ye may be found of him in peace, without spot, and blameless" (2 Peter 3:10-14).

Therefore, Jesus was speaking of the meek who will inherit the *new* earth, where there will be no sin. John the revelator wrote:

"And I saw a new heaven and a new earth: for the first heaven and the first earth were passed away; and there was no more sea. And I John saw the holy city, new Jerusalem, coming down from God out of heaven, prepared as a bride adorned for her husband. And I heard a great voice out of heaven saying, Behold, the tabernacle of God is with men, and he will dwell with them, and they shall be his people, and God himself shall be with them, and be their God" (Rev. 21:1-3).

The new earth is to be the home of God's redeemed people of all ages. God Himself will dwell with them. This world that once was the home of the great rebellion in the universe will become a living testimony of God's love and grace.

The New Jerusalem will be the capital city of the new earth. This beautiful city has a wall of jasper, gates of pearl, and a foundation of precious stones (verses 18-21). The new earth will be a place of no pain or suffering of any kind:

"And God shall wipe away all tears from their eyes; and there shall be no more death, neither sorrow, nor crying, neither shall there be any more pain: for the former things are passed away" (verse 4).

The painful memories of the past will even be healed:

"For, behold, I create new heavens and a new earth: and the former shall not be remembered, nor come into mind" (Isa. 65:17).

John continued describing the New Jerusalem with these words:

"And he shewed me a pure river of water of life, clear as crystal, proceeding out of the throne of God and of the Lamb. In the midst of the street of it, and on either side of the river, was there the tree of life, which bare twelve manner of fruits, and yielded her fruit every month: and the leaves of the tree were for the healing of the nations. And there shall be no more curse: but the throne of God and of the Lamb shall be in it; and his servants shall serve him: and they shall see his face; and his name shall be in their foreheads. . . . And they shall reign for ever and ever" (Rev. 22:1-5).

One thing from this present world that will still be

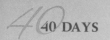

in the new earth is God's holy Sabbath day, which He created at the end of Creation week:

"For as the new heavens and the new earth, which I will make, shall remain before me, saith the Lord, so shall your seed and your name remain. And it shall come to pass, that from one new moon to another, and from one sabbath to another, shall all flesh come to worship before me, saith the Lord" (Isa. 66:22, 23).

Even the animals in this world that are vicious will be tame and peaceful: "The wolf and the lamb shall feed together, and the lion shall eat straw like the bullock. . . . They shall not hurt nor destroy in all my holy mountain, saith the Lord" (Isa. 65:25).

At Christ's second coming the redeemed will receive perfect bodies and minds. They will be changed in the "twinkling of an eye":

"Behold, I shew you a mystery; We shall not all sleep, but we shall all be changed, in a moment, in the twinkling of an eye, at the last trump: for the trumpet shall sound, and the dead shall be raised incorruptible, and we shall be changed. For this corruptible must put on incorruption, and this mortal must put on immortality" (1 Cor. 15:51-53).

God has a glorious future planned for His redeemed. Jesus paid the price for our redemption. It is one thing to know what the Bible teaches about the new earth and the New Jerusalem, but the most important thing is that we have accepted Jesus Christ and truly know Him as our Lord and Savior. For John wrote:

"Blessed are those who wash their robes, that they may have the right to the tree of life and may go through the gates into the city. . . . The Spirit and the bride say, 'Come!' And let him who hears say, 'Come!' Let the one who is thirsty come; and let the one who wishes take the free gift of the water of life" (Rev. 22:14-17, NIV).

Personal Reflection and Discussion

1. What will ultimately happen to this sinful world? _____

2. What is the world called that God creates following the destruction of this sinful earth? _____
_____

3. Describe what the New Jerusalem will be like: _____

4. Describe what the new earth will be like: _____

5. What remains in the new earth that is present in this sinful world? _____
_____

6. Who will inhabit the New Jerusalem and new earth? _____

Prayer Activity

● **Call your prayer partner and discuss the devotional with him or her.**
● **Pray with your prayer partner:**
    (1) for God to baptize you with His Holy Spirit
    (2) for God to continue to bring revival in your life and the church
    (3) to thank God for the New Jerusalem and the new earth He has prepared for you
    (4) for the individuals on your prayer list

Day 31

Exchanging Death for Life

When Adam and Eve fell into sin, they were separated from God. However, God said, "I love you so much I will not let you go." God also knew that if we were to be delivered from our sinful condition, He would have to do it all. For no matter how hard we try to save ourselves, it is an impossible task. All we can do is accept by faith God's provision for our salvation.

Paul describes our hopeless condition in Romans 7:

"For I know that in me (that is, in my flesh,) dwelleth no good thing: for to will is present with me; but how to perform that which is good I find not. . . . I find then a law, that, when I would do good, evil is present with me. For I delight in the law of God after the inward man: but I see another law in my members, warring against the law of my mind, and bringing me into captivity to the law of sin which is in my members. O wretched man that I am! who shall deliver me from the body of this death? . . . God; but with the flesh the law of sin" (Rom. 7:18, 21-25).

Therefore, the first step in escaping our entrapment in sin and making it through earth's final events victoriously is to recognize our utter helplessness to save ourselves. We must accept the fact that not one of us is righteous, for we have all sinned:

"As it is written, There is none righteous, no, not one. . . . For all have sinned, and come short of the glory of God" (Rom. 3:10-23).

Because of this condition we are all condemned to death as unrighteous lawbreakers. This terrible condition came upon humanity through the forefather of us all—Adam:

"Wherefore, as by one man sin entered into the world, and death by sin; and so death passed upon all men, for that all have sinned" (Rom. 5:12).

Therefore, every human being stands before God as a condemned sinner deserving of death. That is our hopeless, helpless condition. But God did something for us so that we would not all be eternally lost and separated from Him.

This is why Elohim, our Creator God (Gen. 1:1), chose to be born a man in the person of Jesus Christ, live a human life, and allow Himself to be put to death. Only Christ, the Son of God, could save humanity (John 1:1-4, 14). When Jesus walked this earth as a man, He lived the perfect, sinless, righteous life (1 Peter 2:22). He was tempted in all points just as we are—but unlike us, He did not falter; He gained for us the victory over every temptation (Heb. 4:15).

However, Christ living a perfectly obedient, righteous life did not do away with the just death penalty that we deserve for our sins. God had to also take that death penalty upon Himself if we were to be free from it. The prophet Isaiah describes how God removed the death penalty from us:

"But he was wounded for our transgressions, he was bruised for our iniquities: the chastisement of our peace was upon him; and with his stripes we are healed. All we like sheep have gone astray; we have turned every one to his own way; and the Lord hath laid on him the iniquity of us all" (Isa. 53:5, 6).

God removed the death penalty from us by becoming one of us, and allowing our sins to be placed on Him on the cross, suffering the death penalty we deserve:

"Let this mind be in you, which was also in Christ Jesus: who, being in the form of God, thought it not robbery to be equal with God: but made himself of no reputation, and took upon him the form of a servant, and

71

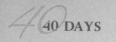

made in the likeness of men: and being found in fashion as a man, he humbled himself, and became obedient unto death, even the death of the cross" (Phil. 2:5-8).

When Jesus took the death penalty upon Himself, He gave us eternal life:

"For the wages of sin is death; but the gift of God is eternal life through Jesus Christ our Lord" (Rom. 6:23).

Since Christ died for our sins, by faith we can accept the free gifts of forgiveness and eternal life Jesus offers to us:

"And this is the record, that God hath given to us eternal life, and this life is in his Son. He that hath the Son hath life; and he that hath not the Son of God hath not life. These things have I written unto you that believe on the name of the Son of God; that ye may know that ye have eternal life, and that ye may believe on the name of the Son of God" (1 John 5:11-13).

By faith in Christ, a marvelous exchange takes place in the Christian. Jesus takes our sins and death penalty upon Himself, and He gives us forgiveness and eternal life. We must experience this exchange in order to be ready for earth's final events.

Personal Reflection and Discussion

1. What was God's attitude toward Adam and Eve after they sinned? _____

_____

2. Can we save ourselves from our sinful condition? _____

_____

3. What just penalty has fallen upon us because of sin? _____

_____

4. How did God save humanity from the just penalty of death? _____

_____

Prayer Activity

● **Call your prayer partner and discuss the devotional with him or her.**
● **Pray with your prayer partner:**
>   **(1) for God to continue to baptize you with the Holy Spirit**
>   **(2) for God to continue to bring revival in your life and in the church**
>   **(3) to thank God for taking your death penalty upon Himself**
>   **(4) to thank God for the forgiveness and eternal life He gives you**
>   **(5) for the individuals on your prayer list**

Day 32

Exchanging Unrighteousness for Righteousness

In yesterday's devotional we read about Jesus dying on the cross for our sins. Because of this we can be forgiven and receive eternal life as a free gift by faith in Christ as our Savior. Today we will consider something else Christ gives to us—His righteousness.

Once we understand our sinful condition we might say, "I now realize I'm a sinner. I accept Christ as my Savior. So I will now begin obeying God's law, try hard not to sin, and become righteous in His sight."

This was the spiritual trap the Jews of Christ's day fell into. They thought they could be righteous in God's sight by simply keeping the law (Rom. 9:31, 32). They were trying the impossible and didn't realize it. So when Christ came preaching righteousness by faith, the religious leaders believed He was teaching heresy. They rejected the only One through whom they could become righteous. The apostle Paul wrote of their condition and clearly stated that Christ is the "end" or fulfillment of the law for righteousness for all who believe in Him:

"Brethren, my heart's desire . . . for Israel is, that they might be saved. For I bear them record that they have a zeal of God, but not according to knowledge. For they being ignorant of God's righteousness, and going about to establish their own righteousness, have not submitted themselves to the righteousness of God. For Christ is the end of the law for righteousness to every one that believeth" (Rom. 10:1-4).

On the other hand, the non-Jews (Gentiles) who accepted Christ attained righteousness before God. How did they do that? They became righteous before God by faith in Christ and His righteousness (Rom. 9:30). For the Bible teaches that there is no way to become righteous and be saved except through belief in Christ (Acts 4:12). No one is made righteous and saved by their own righteous works. Righteousness and salvation come only through faith in Jesus (Titus 3:5, 6). This is why Paul wrote:

"Therefore by the deeds of the law there shall no flesh be justified in his sight. . . . Therefore we conclude that a man is justified by faith without the deeds of the law" (Rom. 3:20-28).

The truth is that when we come to realize we are sinful lawbreakers we are powerless to change that state of being. We are not able to begin keeping the law of God in order to achieve righteousness and freedom from the guilt and penalty of sin in our life, which is called justification. No matter how hard we try to obey God's law, we still fall short of perfect, righteous obedience. We are sinners through and through—slaves to sin through our very nature.

This is why God knew that if He was to save us, He would have to do it all. He would have to come to this world and not only die for our sins but also generate a perfect, human righteousness for us, since we are incapable of developing righteousness for ourselves. Paul understood this when he wrote of his desire to "be found in him, not having mine own righteousness, which is of the law, but that which is through the faith of Christ, the righteousness which is of God by faith" (Phil. 3:9). Hence, God in the person of Jesus Christ came to earth and developed righteousness for us. God then gives us that righteousness when we accept Jesus Christ as our Savior.

The only way we become righteous in God's sight is to ask God to forgive us for our sins and accept

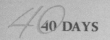

Christ as our Savior from sin: "If we confess our sins, he is faithful and just to forgive us our sins, and to cleanse us from all unrighteousness" (1 John 1:9).

By faith in Christ, a marvelous exchange takes place in the Christian. Jesus takes our sins and death penalty upon Himself and gives us His perfect righteousness and eternal life. Ellen White wrote of this:

"Christ was treated as we deserve, that we might be treated as He deserves. He was condemned for our sins, in which He had no share, that we might be justified by His righteousness, in which we had no share. He suffered the death which was ours, that we might receive the life which was His. 'With His stripes we are healed'" (*The Desire of Ages*, p. 25).

This is why those who are ready to meet Jesus are described as "he that is righteous, let him be righteous still" (Rev. 22:11).

Personal Reflection and Discussion

1. Is it possible for a Christian to become righteous by obeying God's law? _____

_____

2. How did God generate a human righteousness in this world? _____

_____

3. How can the Christian receive Christ's righteousness? _____

_____

4. How did Ellen White describe what Jesus did for you? _____

_____

Prayer Activity

● **Call your prayer partner and discuss the devotional with him or her.**
● **Pray with your prayer partner:**
   (1) for God to continue to baptize you with the Holy Spirit
   (2) for God to continue to bring revival in your life and the church
   (3) for Jesus to forgive you for all your sins and give you His righteousness
   (4) to thank God for coming to this world and generating a human righteousness
   (5) for the individuals on your prayer list

God's Word and Earth's Final Events

Those who make it through the time of trouble and are ready to meet Jesus will definitely be a people of prayer and the Word of God. The Bible will have played a major role in enlightening them of God's will. As the psalmist wrote:

"Thy word is a lamp unto my feet, and a light unto my path" (Ps. 119:105).

God's Word will also protect them from Satan's deceptions:

"He shall cover thee with his feathers, and under his wings shalt thou trust: his truth shall be thy shield and buckler" (Ps. 91:4).

Satan's deceptions will be so effective that Jesus warned: "For there shall arise false Christs, and false prophets, and shall shew great signs and wonders; insomuch that, if it were possible, they shall deceive the very elect" (Matt. 24:24).

Concerning Satan's last-day deceptions and the importance of knowing the truths of God's Word, Ellen White wrote:

"Only those who have been diligent students of the Scriptures and who have received the love of the truth will be shielded from the powerful delusion that takes the world captive. By the Bible testimony these will detect the deceiver in his disguise. To all the testing time will come. By the sifting of temptation the genuine Christian will be revealed. Are the people of God now so firmly established upon his Word that they would not yield to the evidence of their senses? Would they, in such a crisis, cling to the Bible and the Bible only?" (*The Great Controversy*, p. 625).

In their warfare against Satan and his host, God's people will have learned to effectively use the "sword of the Spirit, which is the word of God" (Eph. 6:17). The Greek word translated "word" in this verse is *rhema*, which means "spoken word." They will have learned to defend themselves and carry on the aggressive battle against Satan by speaking God's Word against him.

This is exactly how Jesus gained His victory in the wilderness temptations. In every case, when Satan came against Him with a temptation, it is recorded that "Jesus said" (Matt. 4:4, 7, 10). When Jesus walked this earth He constantly met Satan's attacks with the spoken word. We see this when He cast out devils, healed the sick, and even quelled the storm. When Satan tempted Christ through the words of Peter, the Bible tells us that Jesus responded, "Get thee behind me, Satan" (Matt. 16:23). When we speak God's Word, angels that "excel in strength" come to our aid (Ps. 103:20) and Satan will flee in terror (James 4:7). Believing and saying go hand in hand (Mark 11:23; Rom. 10:9, 10; Rev. 12:11), so understanding and accepting the Word of God is essential in order to avoid the deceptions of the last days. Paul warned us:

"And with all deceivableness of unrighteousness in them that perish; because they received not the love of the truth, that they might be saved. And for this cause God shall send them strong delusion, that they should believe a lie: that they all might be damned who believed not the truth, but had pleasure in unrighteousness" (2 Thess. 2:10-12).

We are in serious danger if we choose to reject the teachings of God's Word. Through God's Spirit living in us and a love for God's Word, we will be ready to meet Jesus. It will be our meditation day and night.

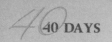

It will be our guide in every aspect of life. We will agree with the psalmist when he wrote that the commandments of God's Word are "more to be desired than gold" and "sweeter also than honey" (Ps. 19:10).

Personal Reflection and Discussion

1. What role will reading God's Word play in helping God's people through earth's final crisis?

_____

_____

2. Who did Ellen White say would avoid Satan's deceptions? _____

_____

3. What did Paul say would happen to those who reject God's truth?_____

_____

4. How precious should God's Word be to the Christian?_____

_____

Prayer Activity

- **Call your prayer partner and discuss the devotional with him or her.**
- **Pray with your prayer partner:**
    - **(1) for God to baptize you with His Holy Spirit**
    - **(2) for God to continue to bring revival in your life and the church**
    - **(3) for Jesus to lead you to become a man or woman of God's Word and have your life firmly founded on it**
    - **(4) for the individuals on your prayer list**

Day 34

Prayer and Earth's Final Events

When we receive the baptism of the Holy Spirit, a deep, inner desire will begin to develop within us, calling us to spend more time in prayer and communion with our heavenly Father. We can either yield to this God-given desire or ignore it. However, if we want to experience the deep things of God and the fullness of Christ in our lives, we must yield to this desire to pray. If we want to see His delivering power manifested in our lives over everything Satan tries to bring on us—especially during earth's final crisis—we must spend much time with God in prayer.

As Christians we have known the importance of prayer for years. Many times we have made efforts to spend time in prayer, but those special seasons of prayer were perhaps motivated by some crisis and didn't continue for very long. Our problem is that we have perceivably become self-sufficient in meeting our own needs and the needs of the church. We have learned to rely on our own efforts to do the work of God. We have been involved in much planning and many programs. We have learned to depend on the "flesh" to do God's work. In mercy, He has blessed our feeble efforts. However, there is a blessing beyond our greatest expectations awaiting us when we receive the baptism of the Holy Spirit and enter the prayer relationship into which He desires to lead us. Only then will our plans be God's plans and our activities be God's activities.

Only that which what the Lord has done through us, and not what we have done in our own wisdom, will have eternal value. Paul wrote of this with the words: "For we are labourers together with God: ye are God's husbandry, ye are God's building. . . . Now if any man build upon this foundation gold, silver, precious stones, wood, hay, stubble; every man's work shall be made

manifest: for the day shall declare it, because it shall be revealed by fire; and the fire shall try every man's work of what sort it is. If any man's work abide which he hath built thereupon, he shall receive a reward. If any man's work shall be burned, he shall suffer loss: but he himself shall be saved; yet so as by fire" (1 Cor. 3:9-15).

Jesus had a meaningful, deep, and powerful relationship with His Father. In fact, this relationship was so close and intimate that Jesus declared that "I and my Father are one" (John 10:30). Everything Jesus did in word and action was under the direction and power of His Father. Jesus emphasized this when He said:

"Believest thou not that I am in the Father, and the Father in me? the words that I speak unto you I speak not of myself: but the Father that dwelleth in me, he doeth the works" (John 14:10).

How did Jesus obtain such a close oneness with His Father? It was through prayer. When Jesus was baptized with water, He prayed (Luke 3:21). In answer to Christ's prayer, the Holy Spirit descended upon Him, and He received this Spirit baptism in answer to prayer. Immediately after, He spent 40 days and nights fasting and praying in the wilderness. From this special communion with His Father, Christ came forth prepared to do the work He came to earth to do. He was empowered to be victorious over Satan.

Time and again we see Christ in prayer during His ministry on earth. After teaching great multitudes and healing them of their infirmities He "withdrew himself into the wilderness, and prayed" (Luke 5:16). Before calling the 12 disciples, He "continued all night in prayer to God" (Luke 6:12). He prayed again on the Mount of Transfiguration (Luke 9:29). Jesus was

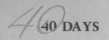

drawn by the Spirit to spend time with His heavenly Father in much prayer, and He responded to this deep, inner need. He knew it was only through such times of prayer that He would be one with the Father and be empowered to do the work He came to do.

Jesus gained His victories over Satan's works through prayer with the Father. When we read of Christ confronting Satan in the lives of men, women, and nature in the forms of devil possession, disease, death, storm, etc., we do not necessarily see Christ at that moment in deep prayer with His Father, praying for the power to deliver. He had already received that power from the Father during consistent times of intimate prayer. When confronted with Satan and his works, Jesus simply spoke the word in the power and authority of the Father, and Satan's power was broken. Christ's word cast out devils, healed the sick, raised the dead, and quelled the storm.

The lesson is clear. Christ maintained His oneness with the Father and received His power over the enemy during His seasons of prayer. He then came away from these prayer times taking the Father with Him. He was conscious of the Father's presence moment by moment and day by day. Christ maintained this conscious and very real oneness with the Father throughout His life. Whenever He was confronted by Satan He was prepared to meet the challenge and gain the victory because of His prayer life. This must also be the experience of God's remnant people, who make it through earth's final crisis victoriously.

Personal Reflection and Discussion

1. What effect will the baptism of the Holy Spirit have on our prayer life? _____
_____

2. How do Christians often conduct God's work? _____
_____

3. Describe Jesus' prayer life: _____
_____

4. What kind of prayer life is needed by God's remnant people? _____
_____

Prayer Activity

- **Call your prayer partner and discuss the devotional with him or her.**
- **Pray with your prayer partner:**
    - **(1) for God to baptize you with His Holy Spirit**
    - **(2) for God to bring revival in your life and in the church**
    - **(3) for Jesus to lead you to become a man or woman of prayer**
    - **(4) for the individuals on your prayer list**

Day 35

Fellowship and Earth's Final Events

The book of Acts describes the Christians in the first century. An enlightening verse is found in Acts 2:

"And they continued stedfastly in the apostles' doctrine and fellowship, and in breaking of bread, and in prayers" (verse 42).

Here we read that fellowship was an important element in their Christian experience.

The Greek word translated "fellowship" is *koinonia*. The noun form of this term means to share in, participate in, or to be actively involved in. The verb form means to communicate, distribute, and impart. In essence, *koinonia* means ministering to one another. It means sharing one another's hopes, dreams, struggles, and pains. The early Spirit-filled Christians allowed God to minister through them to one another. Their love for one another was so great that "all that believed were together, and had all things common; and sold their possessions and goods, and parted them to all men, as every man had need" (Acts 2:44, 45).

We weren't created to stand alone in this world. It is in genuine Christian fellowship that the gifts of the Spirit function, for the building up of the body of Christ—the church. Christians are to minister to one another and pray for one another in the Spirit:

"Praying always with all prayer and supplication in the Spirit, and watching thereunto with all perseverance and supplication for all saints" (Eph. 6:18).

Christian fellowship played an important role in the advancement of the gospel in the early church. It will also play an important role in the finishing of God's work prior to Christ's return. The mutual prayers for one another and words of encouragement will be used by the Spirit to strengthen God's remnant people during earth's final events. Concerning this, James wrote:

"Confess your faults one to another, and pray one for another, that ye may be healed. The effectual fervent prayer of a righteous man availeth much" (James 5:16).

Ellen White adds:

"Although God dwells not in temples made with hands, yet He honors with His presence the assemblies of His people. He has promised that when they come together to seek Him, to acknowledge their sins, and to pray for one another, He will meet with them by His Spirit" (*The Faith I Live By*, p. 62).

Fellowship facilitates united prayer, which increases the power of prayer. The Old Testament taught this increased effectiveness when God's people unite against the enemy:

"And five of you shall chase an hundred, and an hundred of you shall put ten thousand to flight" (Lev. 26:8).

"Though one may be overpowered, two can defend themselves. A cord of three strands is not quickly broken" (Eccl. 4:12, NIV).

Jesus taught the importance of fellowshipping together as believers:

"Again I say unto you, That if two of you shall agree on earth as touching any thing that they shall ask, it shall be done for them of my Father which is in heaven. For where two or three are gathered together in my name, there am I in the midst of them" (Matt. 18:19, 20).

Ellen White described many of the closing events of earth's history in *The Great Controversy*. Regard-

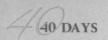

ing the time when evil men are about to destroy God's people from the face of the earth, she wrote:

"With shouts of triumph, jeering, and imprecation, throngs of evil men are about to rush upon their prey, when, lo, a dense blackness, deeper than the darkness of the night, falls upon the earth. Then a rainbow, shining with the glory from the throne of God, spans the heavens and seems to encircle each praying company. The angry multitudes are suddenly arrested. Their mocking cries die away. The objects of their murderous rage are forgotten. With fearful forebodings they gaze upon the symbol of God's covenant and long to be shielded from its overpowering brightness" (pp. 635, 636).

Note that she used the words "each praying company." God's people will be gathered into many "praying companies," or fellowship groups, during earth's final crisis (time of trouble) as their lives are threatened. These fellowship groups will play an essential role in their victory over the enemy during that trying time.

Personal Reflection and Discussion

1. What were four characteristics of first-century Christians described in Acts 2:42?_____
_____

2. What does the Greek word translated "fellowship" in the New Testament mean?_____
_____

3. Why is it important that a Christian be involved in a Spirit-filled fellowship group? _____
_____

4. What did Ellen White write about fellowship groups during the time of trouble? _____
_____

Prayer Activity

- **Call your prayer partner and discuss the devotional with him or her.**
- **Pray with your prayer partner:**
    - **(1) for God to baptize you with His Holy Spirit**
    - **(2) for God to bring revival in your life and in the church**
    - **(3) for Jesus to lead you into meaningful fellowship with other Christians**
    - **(4) for the individuals on your prayer list**

Day 36

Experiencing God's Love

It is most important that we experience God's love for us if we are to enter into the deliverance He offers. It is not enough for us to have merely a "head knowledge" that God loves us. Rather, we must come to know God's love for us on the deepest level of our being. The fullest deliverance from the influences of Satan in our life is dependent on knowing this. Paul points this out when he wrote his prayer for the believers in Ephesus:

"That he would grant you, according to the riches of his glory, to be strengthened with might by his Spirit in the inner man; that Christ may dwell in your hearts by faith; that ye, being rooted and grounded in love, may be able to comprehend with all saints what is the breadth, and length, and depth, and height; and to know the love of Christ, which passeth knowledge, that ye might be filled with all the fulness of God. Now unto him that is able to do exceeding abundantly above all that we ask or think, according to the power that worketh in us" (Eph. 3:16-20).

Why is knowing that God loves us so important? John tells us in his first letter:

"We love him, because he first loved us" (1 John 4:19).

We can love God only to the degree that we know His love for us. The more we know deep within ourselves that God loves and accepts us, the stronger our love for Him will be. Love begets love. This is why the baptism of the Holy Spirit is so essential. It is only through the Spirit's infilling that the "love of God is shed abroad in our hearts" (Rom. 5:5). It is only by the baptism of the Holy Spirit that we experience the fruits of the Spirit (Gal. 5:22, 23). The first fruit listed is "love." Once this divine love begins to be experienced, the other fruit can begin to grow. The greater we experience God's love for us, the deeper we experience emotional healing. The deeper our experience of emotional healing, the greater will we experience joy, peace, patience, gentleness, goodness, faith, meekness, and self-control. God has provided a way for us to be delivered from anger, bitterness, jealousy, critical attitudes, etc.

John gives us another important insight:

"He who loveth God [loveth] his brother also" (1 John 4:21).

Our experiencing God's love is essential for us to truly love one another. We will love our brothers and sisters in Christ only to the degree that we know God's love for us, and to the degree that we love God. You and I cannot make ourselves love others; only God can do that through us. And He does this by leading us to experience His love for us to the fullest.

How does "knowing" God loves and accepts us heal us emotionally? John again gives us the answer:

"There is no fear in love; but perfect love casteth out fear: because fear hath torment. He that feareth is not made perfect in love" (verse 18).

When we know in our deepest, inmost being that God really loves and accepts us, our fears begin to dissolve or be "cast out." Why is it important that fear be cast out? Because the root cause of our emotional pain is fear. The painful experiences we have gone through have caused us to feel fear of rejection, fear of abandonment, fear of failure, etc. When this fear is gone, the way is open for us to experience the greatest healing. We can then experience Christ's joy (John 15:11),

81

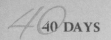

which bring great inner strength because "the joy of the Lord is your strength" (Neh. 8:10).

When fear is cast out, stress is alleviated—worry and anxiety are gone. The way is then prepared for us to experience emotional, spiritual, and even physical healing, for many of our physical ills are closely related to our emotional pain. When God's love casts out our fears, Christ's peace can be ours (John 14:27).

Jesus said, "If ye love me, keep my commandments" (verse 15). We can keep the commandments in love only to the degree that we know God loves us. Those who remain faithful to God during earth's final crisis will do so because they know God loves them, and they love God in return. They will not be faithful to a law that says to keep holy the Sabbath simply because the law says to do so. No, they will obey God's fourth commandment because they love Him, and don't want to do anything that will hurt Him or damage their relationship with Him. They want to be faithful to a God who they know loves them, and who they truly love in return.

Note: See Appendix E to read your heavenly Father's love letter to you as revealed in His Word.

Personal Reflection and Discussion

1. What does Paul say that knowing God loves them will do for Christians? _____

_____

2. What relationship is there between knowing God loves us and us loving God in return? _____

_____

3. What relationship is there between knowing God loves us and us loving others?_____

_____

4. What will be the motive that enables God's remnant people to obey Him? _____

_____

Prayer Activity

● **Call your prayer partner and discuss the devotional with him or her.**
● **Pray with your prayer partner:**
    (1) for God to baptize you with His Holy Spirit
    (2) for God to bring revival in your life and in the church
    (3) for God to reveal His love for you
    (4) for the individuals on your prayer list

Day 37

The Importance of Health Principles

Satan has sought to lead humanity to divert from God's laws of physical health. Since the 1960s he has worked hard to bring illicit drugs into society. Such drugs affect the mind and body. Why is Satan attacking the mind so fiercely? Because he knows earth's final events are fast approaching, and he wants to do everything he can to hinder humanity from experiencing God. As we have seen in this devotional, those who make it through the time of trouble victoriously and are ready for Christ's return will have to have an extremely close relationship with Jesus Christ and let Him live out His righteous obedience in and through them.

We are created as physical beings. God does not communicate with us magically or in a way separate from our physical body. He communicates with us and influences us through our own mind. Therefore, whatever physically affects our brain will affect God's ability to influence and communicate with us.

Ellen White understood the importance of the brain in relation to God's communication with us when she wrote:

"The brain nerves which communicate with the entire system are the only medium through which Heaven can communicate with man and affect his inmost life. Whatever disturbs the circulation of the electric currents in the nervous system lessens the strength of the vital powers, and the result is a deadening of the sensibilities of the mind" (*My Life Today*, p. 148).

Our physical health habits will affect the function of our brains. Therefore it is important to understand the laws of our being and how to cooperate with God in achieving optimum health. Ellen White listed some of these laws of health in the following statement:

"Pure air, sunlight, abstemiousness, rest, exercise, proper diet, the use of water, trust in divine power—these are the true remedies" (*The Ministry of Healing*, p. 127).

When these and other laws of health are practiced, God will be better able to communicate with us because our brains will be in better health.

"The brain is the organ and instrument of the mind, and controls the whole body. In order for the other parts of the system to be healthy, the brain must be healthy. And in order for the brain to be healthy, the blood must be pure. If by correct habits of eating and drinking the blood is kept pure, the brain will be properly nourished" (Ellen G. White, *Medical Ministry*, p. 291).

Shortly before Jesus returns, God's glory will be seen in this earth. The last generation of Christians will perfectly reflect the character of Christ:

"And after these things I saw another angel come down from heaven, having great power; and the earth was lightened with his glory" (Rev. 18:1).

Therefore the purpose of maintaining good physical health is so Christ can live out His life in us, which enables His character to be most fully reflected in our life. Paul described the Christian life when he wrote:

"I am crucified with Christ: nevertheless I live; yet not I, but Christ liveth in me: and the life which I now live in the flesh I live by the faith of the Son of God, who loved me, and gave himself for me" (Gal. 2:20).

Those ready to meet Jesus will be like Him:

"Beloved, now are we the sons of God, and it doth not yet appear what we shall be: but we know that,

83

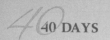

when he shall appear, we shall be like him; for we shall see him as he is" (1 John 3:2).

The reason for this is that it is Jesus manifested in them. This is what Christ is waiting to take place in His followers. The total health message will play an important role in this manifestation in the lives of His children. Ellen White warned us as to what happens when these laws of health are ignored:

"By the indulgence of perverted appetite, man loses his power to resist temptation" (*The Ministry of Healing*, p. 335).

Personal Reflection and Discussion

1. Why has Satan sought to lead humanity away from God's laws of health? _____
_____

2. How does God communicate with people? _____
_____

3. What are some of the laws of health that make it easier for God to clearly communicate with us? _
_____

4. How will disregarding health laws affect those who are preparing for Christ's return? _____
_____

5. How does the Bible describe those who are ready for Christ's return? _____
_____

Prayer Activity

● **Call your prayer partner and discuss this devotional with him or her.**
● **Pray with your prayer partner:**
    (1) for God to baptize you with His Holy Spirit
    (2) for God to bring revival in your life and in the church
    (3) for God to help you understand the seriousness of following His health laws
    (4) for the individuals on your prayer list

Day 38

Spirit Baptism and Righteousness by Faith Required

It is one thing to understand the antichrist beast power's identity and his mark, but it is another thing to be prepared for earth's final events, which include the enforcement of that mark. One can know what the Bible teaches on these prophecies and yet still be unprepared to be faithful to God when they are fulfilled.

The baptism of the Holy Spirit is an experience that every Christian must have who is living at the time the mark of the beast is enforced. Just as Jesus needed to be filled with the Spirit before He faced His greatest temptations in the wilderness (Luke 3:21, 22; 4:1-13), so also must the Christian be Spirit-filled in order to face the temptations of earth's final events. Ellen White confirmed this:

"Nothing but the baptism of the Holy Spirit can bring up the church to its right position, and prepare the people of God for the fast approaching conflict" (*Manuscript Releases*, vol. 2, p. 30).

It is through the empowerment of the Holy Spirit that God's people receive the strength to remain faithful to Him under such trying circumstances. Paul told us that our inner selves are strengthened by the Spirit (Eph. 3:16).

Another necessary experience for each Christian living when the mark of the beast is enforced is to have learned how to let Jesus live out His life of victory within him or her. God's followers must experience righteousness by faith in Christ alone, and to the fullest extent. This experience will enable the believer to truly keep all of God's commandments. That is why Ellen White connected the message of righteousness by faith with commandment-keeping. She wrote about the blessing of righteousness by faith that the Lord brought to our denomination in 1888, as well as its relationship to obeying God's commandments:

"The Lord in His great mercy sent a most precious message to His people through Elders Waggoner and Jones. This message was to bring more prominently before the world the uplifted Savior, the sacrifice for the sins of the whole world. It presented justification through faith in the Surety; it invited the people to receive the righteousness of Christ, *which is made manifest in obedience to all the commandments of God*" (*Testimonies to Ministers,* pp. 91, 92; italics supplied).

As we fully receive Christ into our life through the baptism of the Holy Spirit and learn to experience righteousness by faith in Christ alone in our obedience, commandment-keeping will be the natural result. This is why baptism of the Holy Spirit and righteousness by faith must also be presented when the third angel's message is preached, warning the world of the antichrist and the mark of the beast.

When individuals respond positively to the third angel's message, they need to understand how to let Jesus live out His obedience in and through them. Their obedience will then be from the heart and not legalistic. The love of God will be so planted in their heart (Rom. 5:5) that they would rather die than hurt Jesus by their actions. Their one desire will be to remain faithful to Christ and properly represent Him before the world. This is how the earth will be lightened with God's glory in the end, just before Jesus returns (Rev. 18:1). God is calling each one of us to be a part of that people.

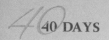

Personal Reflection and Discussion

1. Is knowing what the Bible teaches about earth's final events all that is necessary in order to be ready for those events? _____

_____

_____

2. Why is it important to understand and experience the baptism of the Holy Spirit in order to be ready for earth's final events? _____

_____

_____

3. Why is it necessary to understand and experience righteousness by faith in Christ alone in order to be ready for earth's final events? _____

_____

_____

4. Why is simply preaching the third angel's message not enough to prepare individuals for earth's final events? _____

_____

_____

Prayer Activity

- **Call your prayer partner and discuss the devotional with him or her.**
- **Pray with your prayer partner:**
     (1) for God to continue to baptize you with the Holy Spirit
     (2) for God to continue to bring revival in your life and the church
     (3) for God to enable you to understand and experience righteousness by faith in Christ alone, in order to be ready for earth's final events
     (4) for the individuals on your prayer list

The Mystery of God Finished

Just before Jesus returns to deliver His people, the "mystery of God" will be finished:

"But in the days of the voice of the seventh angel, when he shall begin to sound, the mystery of God should be finished, as he hath declared to his servants the prophets" (Rev. 10:7).

What is this "mystery of God" that is to be finished? Paul tells us in Colossians 1:26, 27:

"The mystery which hath been hid from ages and from generations, but now is made manifest to his saints: to whom God would make known what is the riches of the glory of this mystery among the Gentiles; which is *Christ in you*, the hope of glory."

The mystery of God is what the baptism of the Holy Spirit and righteousness by faith are all about—Christ in you, which is your only hope of reflecting God's glory. The "mystery of God" is the gospel of a sin-pardoning and sin-delivering Savior. That is why Jesus was named "Jesus." He was sent to "save His people from their sins," not *in* their sins (Matt. 1:21). The "mystery of God" is full justification and sanctification through Jesus Christ. It is righteousness by faith in Christ alone.

This is the mystery that will be completed in God's people at the very end of time. This is the mystery that will enable God's last remnant people to fulfill their mission. That is why God is bringing this message to His people at this hour of earth's history. We place ourselves in grave jeopardy if we reject God's merciful call to understand and experience the baptism of the Holy Spirit, and Christ's justifying and sanctifying righteousness.

I personally believe that today there will be a remnant among God's professed people who will respond to God's call and experience the full and complete deliverance Christ offers. They will be the ones who receive benefit from the latter rain of the Spirit. They will be those who give the loud cry of the third angel's message in great power. They will be the ones who make it through the time of trouble or tribulation victoriously by being faithful to God and not receiving the mark of the beast. And they will be the ones who will stand in the very presence of Christ, in all His glory, and not be consumed.

We have seen in this devotional that God is giving a very serious warning to last-day Laodicean Christians. They must come out of their Laodicean condition in order to be ready for Christ's return. God's message to the Laodiceans also gives us the answer. Jesus indicates He is standing at the door and wants to come in (Rev. 3:20). How do we let Him in? Through the baptism of the Holy Spirit (John 14:16-18; 1 John 3:24).

What will the baptism of the Holy Spirit do for a "lukewarm" Christian? The infilling of God's Spirit will bring revival to the recipient, which is the only answer to Laodicea's problem. Only by revival will the church come to a spiritual condition that will allow God to use it in a mighty way, as a means of delivering people from the powers of darkness.

Ellen White recognized the urgency of revival when she wrote:

"A revival of true godliness among us is the greatest and most urgent of all our needs. To seek this should be our first work" (*Selected Messages*, book 1, p. 121).

She also understood the relationship between revival and receiving the baptism of the Holy Spirit:

"The baptism of the Holy Ghost as on the day of Pentecost will lead to a revival of true religion and to

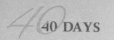

the performance of many wonderful works" (*ibid.*, book 2, p. 57).

The baptism of the Holy Spirit gives the Laodicean Christian the required power to be revived spiritually and to powerfully witness for Christ. Jesus certainly knew the importance of what would happen when the Holy Spirit would be poured out in "early rain" power on the day of Pentecost:

"I have come to bring fire on the earth, and how I wish it were already kindled!" (Luke 12:49, NIV).

What fire was Jesus speaking of? The fire of the Holy Spirit (Luke 3:16).

How does the Laodicean Christian receive the baptism of the Holy Spirit and experience revival? The same way believers always have—by prayerfully claiming God's promise. The baptism of the Holy Spirit was received by the early church on the day of Pentecost as a result of uniting and praying for 10 days, claiming Christ's promise (Acts 1:4-14). Ellen White confirmed this when she wrote:

"A revival need be expected only in answer to prayer" (*ibid.*, book 1, p. 121).

Every Christian today needs to pray the prayer of David:

"Wilt thou not revive us again: that thy people may rejoice in thee?" (Ps. 85:6).

Ellen White told of the process by which the Holy Spirit offers defense against Satan:

"There is nothing that Satan fears so much as that the people of God shall clear the way by removing every hindrance, so that the Lord can pour out His Spirit upon a languishing church and an impenitent congregation" (*ibid.*, p. 124).

Personal Reflection and Discussion

1. According to Revelation 10:7, what will God do as the seventh angel begins to sound? _____

_____

2. According to Colossians 1:27, what is the "mystery of God"? _____

_____

3. How is the baptism of the Holy Spirit and righteousness by faith related to the "mystery of God"?

_____

_____

4. What two Christian experiences did Ellen White say would bring a revival? _____

_____

Prayer Activity

● **Call your prayer partner and discuss the devotional with him or her.**
● **Pray with your prayer partner:**
  (1) for God to continue to baptize you with the Holy Spirit
  (2) for God to continue to bring revival in your life and the church
  (3) for the "mystery of God" to be completed in your life
  (4) for the individuals on your prayer list

Day 40

With God

You were created to have a close, meaningful, intimate relationship with God. Satan hates God and has devised a plan to take you away from Him on this earth and eternally separate you from Him. He led Adam and Eve into sin, which led to separation from God.

In Genesis 3, when we read of Adam and Eve's actions immediately following their fall into sin, we see the instant separation from God that their sin caused:

"And they heard the voice of the Lord God walking in the garden in the cool of the day: and Adam and his wife hid themselves from the presence of the Lord God amongst the trees of the garden" (verse 8).

Sin caused Adam and Eve to run from God and attempt to hide from Him. But in this account of Adam and Eve's sin we find that God immediately sought out the frightened pair:

"And the Lord God called unto Adam, and said unto him, Where art thou?" (verse 9). Adam replied, "I heard thy voice in the garden, and I was afraid, because I was naked; and I hid myself" (verse 10).

Ever since the fall of Adam into sin God has sought to bring humanity back into a close, intimate relationship with Himself. Being reconciled to God is what the plan of salvation is all about. We were created to be with God, but sin separated us from Him. Fortunately, Jesus has made it possible for us to return to God and be with Him eternally.

Throughout the story of God's efforts to return us to Himself, He is the One who constantly seeks to bring us back. It must be that way because our sin has caused us to desire sin rather than God:

"The wicked, through the pride of his countenance, will not seek after God: God is not in all his thoughts" (Ps. 10:4).

"As it is written, There is none righteous, no, not one: there is none that understandeth, there is none that seeketh after God" (Rom. 3:10, 11).

Since our sinfulness made us incapable of initiating our return to an intimate relationship with God, He took it upon Himself to come to us in the person of Jesus Christ. John describes God stepping down from His throne in order to restore our lost relationship with Him:

"In the beginning was the Word, and the Word was with God, and the Word was God. The same was in the beginning with God. All things were made by him; and without him was not any thing made that was made" (John 1:1-3).

"And the Word was made flesh, and dwelt among us, (and we beheld his glory, the glory as of the only begotten of the Father,) full of grace and truth" (verse 14).

Elohim, the very God who created us (Gen. 1:1), became human in order to save us. You are that important to God. John further describes our lost, sinful condition and what God did to restore us back to Himself:

"For God so loved the world, that he gave his only begotten Son, that whosoever believeth in him should not perish, but have everlasting life. For God sent not his Son into the world to condemn the world; but that the world through him might be saved. He that believeth on him is not condemned: but he that believeth not is condemned already, because he hath not believed in the name of the only begotten Son of God" (John 3:16-18).

It's all about being "with God." Do you remember Jesus' response to the thief on the cross, who asked that Jesus remember him when He came into His kingdom? Jesus replied, "You will be *with* me in paradise" (Luke 23:43, NIV).

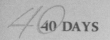

Paul proclaimed that when Jesus returns He will save His redeemed people, and they shall forever be "*with* the Lord" (1 Thess. 4:17).

God loves you so much that He has done everything necessary for you to be with Him forever. He longs to have a close, intimate relationship with you—not only here, but throughout eternity. This is also why He has given to His children the prophecies you have studied in this devotional. He wants you to understand the issues in these last days so you can be prepared and make the right decisions in your life. He does not want you to be deceived and lost. He wants you to be ready to come home when Jesus returns to earth.

It's amazing but true: God has made it possible, even in this sinful world, for you to enter into a close, intimate, meaningful relationship with Him. How can this happen? It happens as you daily experience the baptism of the Holy Spirit, which enables Christ to most fully live in you. It happens as you look to Jesus, who lives in you to give you His victory when you are tempted.

Those ready to meet Jesus will be like Enoch, who "walked with God: and he was not; for God took him" (Gen. 5:24). God's last remnant people will be walking with God, and they will not be found on Planet Earth for 1,000 years because God will "take them," also.

Personal Reflection and Discussion

1. What is Satan's attitude toward God, and what plan did he devise because of this attitude? _____
_____

2. What did Adam and Eve do immediately after they sinned? _____
_____

3. What did God do immediately following Adam and Eve's sin? _____
_____

4. Why does God have to take the initiative to save us? _____
_____

5. What promise did Jesus make to the thief on the cross, and do you think He makes the same promise to you? _____
_____

Prayer Activity

● **Call your prayer partner and discuss the devotional with him or her.**
● **Pray with your prayer partner:**
   (1) for God to reveal to you how special you are to Him
   (2) for God to continue to baptize you with His Spirit every day
   (3) for God to continue to bring revival in your life and in the church
   (4) to thank God for making it possible for you to return to an intimate relationship with Him
   (5) to thank God for the prophecies of His Word that shield you from deception
   (6) for the individuals on your prayer list

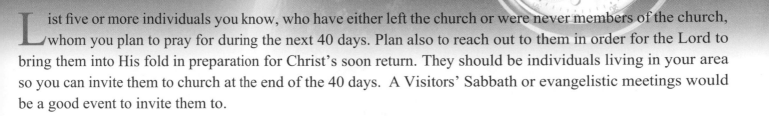

Appendix A

Daily Prayer List

List five or more individuals you know, who have either left the church or were never members of the church, whom you plan to pray for during the next 40 days. Plan also to reach out to them in order for the Lord to bring them into His fold in preparation for Christ's soon return. They should be individuals living in your area so you can invite them to church at the end of the 40 days. A Visitors' Sabbath or evangelistic meetings would be a good event to invite them to.

_____

_____

_____

_____

_____

_____

_____

_____

_____

_____

- **Pray for these individuals every day, claiming the scriptures below on their behalf. These are taken from the *Praying Church Source Book*, pages 128, 129:**
    1. **Pray that God will draw them to Him (John 6:44).**
    2. **Pray that they will seek to know God (Acts 17:27).**
    3. **Pray that they will believe the Word of God (1 Thess. 2:13).**
    4. **Pray that Satan will be bound from blinding them to the truth and that his influences in their life will be "cast down" (2 Cor. 4:4; 10:4, 5).**
    5. **Pray that the Holy Spirit will work in them (John 16:8-13).**
    6. **Pray that they will turn from sin (Acts 3:19).**
    7. **Pray that they will believe in Christ as Savior (John 1:12).**
    8. **Pray that they will obey Christ as Lord (Matt. 7:21).**
    9. **Pray that they will take root and grow in Christ (Col. 2:6, 7).**

- **Prayerfully use the Activities to Show You Care (see Appendix B) list to determine what the Lord wants you to do to reach out to those on your prayer list during the next 40 days. Also, be sure to pray every day for the Visitors' Sabbath and/or evangelistic meetings, if these activities are planned for the end of the 40-day program.**

Appendix B

Activities to Show You Care

The following are suggestions of things you can do for those on your prayer list to show that you care for them. Add to this list as the Lord leads.

1. Call to say what you appreciate about them.
2. Mail a card sharing what God put in your heart to tell them.
3. Send a piece of encouraging literature.
4. Call and pray with them.
5. Invite them to your home for a meal.
6. Invite them to go out to lunch with you.
7. Send a birthday card.
8. Send a card expressing encouragement.
9. Take them a homemade treat.
10. Invite them to go somewhere, such as the mall, a museum, a park, etc.
11. Send a get-well or sympathy card when needed.
12. Give their child a birthday card and gift when appropriate.
13. Invite them to attend church with you.
14. At the appropriate time, ask if they would like to receive Bible studies.
15. _____
16. _____
17. _____
18. _____
19. _____
20. _____

If a Visitors' Sabbath and/or evangelistic meetings are planned at the completion of the 40 days, be sure to invite those on your prayer list to these events.

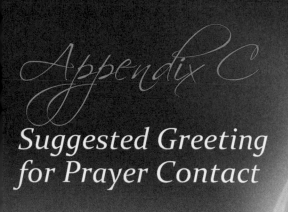

Appendix C

Suggested Greeting for Prayer Contact

Hello, _____ (*interest's name*).

This is _____ (*your name*).

My church is having a special emphasis on prayer and is requesting that we choose five individuals to pray for during the next 40 days.

I have chosen you as one of my five to pray for.

What would you like for me to especially pray for on your behalf? (*For example: family, job, a health issue, etc.*)

(*Write down what they want you to pray for.*)

_____

_____

_____

_____

I appreciate the opportunity to pray for you during the next 40 days.

Thanks, _____ (*interest's name*). I'll keep in touch.

Appendix D

After the 40 Days of Prayer and Devotional Studies

Now that you have completed this 40 days of prayer and devotional studies, you probably don't want the experience you are having with the Lord and the fellowship you are enjoying to fade away. So what should you do next?

One possibility is to go through one of the other 40 Days devotional books:

- *40 Days: Prayers and Devotions to Prepare for the Second Coming* (book 1)
- *40 Days: Prayers and Devotions to Revive Your Experience With God* (book 2)
- *40 Days: God's Health Principles for His Last-Day People* (book 3)

Each book presents biblical teachings that are essential for God's people to understand to be ready for Christ's second coming.

Another possibility is that you begin studying in greater detail the subjects presented in this devotional. Many books in the Adventist Book Centers, as well as the books listed on my Web site, www.spiritbaptism.org, discuss these subjects. My book *Spirit Baptism & Earth's Final Events* focuses especially on the closing events of earth's history and the spiritual experience God's last-day people must have.

If this is your desire, I would suggest you continue meeting with your prayer partner. You may also want to invite others to join you to become a study/prayer fellowship group. This will enable the Lord to strengthen the experience with Him that He has begun in your life during the past 40 days.

Second, continue to pray for those on your prayer list and reach out to them. Also, add others to your list as the Lord leads, and as a group, consider activities to plan to invite those on the prayer lists to attend.

Many who have studied the *40 Days* books have become involved in conference calls, fellowship, and prayer groups. This is proving to be an effective way to daily connect with fellow believers. Great blessings are being received by those who participate in these conference calls.

The devotional can also be an effective means for reaching out to a former or inactive church member. Personally contact them and invite them to go through the *40 Days* devotional with you. If they agree, give them a copy of the book and schedule a time to daily review the devotional with them and to pray with them.

Studying the *40 Days* devotional with newly baptized members following evangelistic meetings is an excellent way to strengthen their personal spiritual life, develop a close fellowship with them, and to connect them to the church in a meaningful way.

Christ wants personal, daily devotional study, prayer, fellowship, as well as reaching out to others to become an integral part of every Christian's life. If this aspect of your life ends with the 40 days of prayer and devotional study, you will not grow into the fullness of Christ that He desires you to experience. Also, regular prayer and devotion is the only way to be ready for Christ's soon return, for it is the only way our intimate relationship with Christ develops. May the Lord abundantly bless your continued devotional study and prayer time with Him, and your efforts to share Him with others.

*Father's Love Letter**

My Child,

You may not know Me, but I know everything about you *(Psalm 139:1)*. I know when you sit down and when you rise up *(Psalm 139:2)*. I am familiar with all your ways *(Psalm 139:3)*. Even the very hairs on your head are numbered *(Matthew 10:29-31)*. For you were made in My image *(Genesis 1:27)*. In Me you live and move and have your being *(Acts 17:28)*. For you are My offspring *(Acts 17:28)*. I knew you even before you were conceived *(Jeremiah 1:4, 5)*. I chose you when I planned creation *(Ephesians 1:11, 12)*. You were not a mistake, for all your days are written in My Book *(Psalm 139:15, 16)*. I determined the exact time of your birth and where you would live *(Acts 17:26)*. You are fearfully and wonderfully made *(Psalm 139:14)*. I knit you together in your mother's womb *(Psalm 139:13)* and brought you forth on the day you were born *(Psalm 71:6)*.

I have been misrepresented by those who don't know Me *(John 8:41-44)*. I am not distant and angry, but I am the complete expression of love *(1 John 4:16)*, and it is my desire to lavish My love on you *(1 John 3:1)* simply because you are My child, and I am your Father *(1 John 3:1)*. I offer you more than your earthly father ever could *(Matthew 7:11)*, for I am the perfect Father *(Matthew 5:48)*. Every good gift that you receive comes from My hand *(James 1:17)*, for I am your provider, and I meet all your needs *(Matthew 6:31-33)*. My plan for your future has always been filled with hope *(Jeremiah 29:11)*, because I love you with an everlasting love *(Jeremiah 31:3)*. My thoughts toward you are as countless as the sand on the seashore *(Psalm 139:17, 18)*, and I rejoice over you with singing *(Zephaniah 3:17)*. I will never stop doing good to you *(Jeremiah*

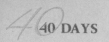

32:40), for you are My treasured possession *(Exodus 19:5)*. I desire to establish you with all My heart and all My soul *(Jeremiah 32:41)*, and I want to show you great and marvelous things *(Jeremiah 33:3)*.

If you seek Me with all your heart, you will find Me *(Deuteronomy 4:29)*. Delight in Me, and I will give you the desires of your heart *(Psalm 37:4)*, for it is I who gave you those desires *(Philippians 2:13)*. I am able to do more for you than you could possibly imagine *(Ephesians 3:20)*, for I am your greatest encourager *(2 Thessalonians 2:16, 17)*. I am also the Father who comforts you in all your troubles *(2 Corinthians 1:3, 4)*. When you are brokenhearted, I am close to you *(Psalm 34:18)*. As a shepherd carries a lamb, I have carried you close to my heart *(Isaiah 40:11)*.

One day I will wipe away every tear from your eyes *(Revelation 21:3, 4)*, and I'll take away all the pain you have suffered on this earth *(Revelation 21:3, 4)*. I am your Father, and I love you even as I love My Son, Jesus *(John 17:23)*, for in Jesus My love for you is revealed *(John 17:26)*. He is the exact representation of My being *(Hebrews 1:3)*. He came to demonstrate that I am for you, not against you *(Romans 8:3)*, and to tell you that I am not counting your sins *(2 Corinthians 5:18, 19)*. Jesus died so that you and I could be reconciled *(2 Corinthians 5:18, 19)*. His death was the ultimate expression of My love for you *(1 John 4:10)*. I gave up everything I loved that I might gain your love *(Romans 8:31, 32)*. If you receive the gift of My Son, Jesus, you receive Me *(1 John 2:23)*, and nothing will ever separate you from My love again *(Romans 8:38, 39)*. Come home, and I'll throw the biggest party heaven has ever seen *(Luke 15:7)*. I have always been Father, and will always be Father *(Ephesians 3:14, 15)*. My question is . . . Will you be My child? *(John 1:12, 13)*.

I am waiting for you *(Luke 15:11-32)*.

Love,
Your Dad, Almighty God